W9-BBS-306

New England's Best Bed & Breakfasts

4th Edition

Delightful Places to Stay
Wonderful Things to Do
When You Get There

Fodor's Travel Publications, Inc.
New York • Toronto • London • Sydney • Auckland
www.fodors.com/

New England's Best Bed & Breakfasts

Editor: Laura M. Kidder

Editorial Contributors: Dorothy Antczak, Michelle Bodak, Paula J. Flanders, Carolyn B. Heller, Hilary Nangle, Anne Peracca, Alan W. Petrucelli, Kevin D. Weaver

Editorial Production: Tracy Patruno

Maps: David Lindroth, *cartographer;* Robert Blake, *map editor*

Design: Fabrizio La Rocca, *creative director;* Guido Caroti, *cover design;* Jolie Novak, *photo editor;* Alida Beck, *illustrator (inns);* Karl Tanner, *illustrator (chapter art)*

Production/Manufacturing: Mike Costa

Cover Photograph: Donovan Reese

Special Sales

Contributors

Freelance writer **Dorothy Antczak** *vacationed in Provincetown, Massachusetts, one year and never left. From her perch on the fist of the arm that is the Cape, Dorothy updated the Nantucket and lower Cape sections.*

Nutmeg State updater **Michelle Bodak** *lives in Milford, Connecticut, and is an associate editor at* Connecticut *magazine. She writes about all aspects of life in the state, as well as travel in New England and the Caribbean ('cause there's nothing like a little contrast to give a writer perspective).*

Though originally from Maine, Granite State updater **Paula J. Flanders** *has lived in New Hampshire for 16 years, ever since she married a New Hampshire native who wouldn't move. She's come to love both the people and the scenery in her adopted state. She is a contributing travel editor for* New Hampshire Living *magazine, and she writes about travel, crafts, and antiques for publications throughout the United States.*

Travel writer **Carolyn B. Heller** *lives in Cambridge, Massachusetts. Her work has appeared in the* Boston Globe, *the* Miami Herald, *the* Philadelphia Inquirer, *and the* Newark Star-Ledger *as well as in* Transitions Abroad *magazine and the book* Travelers' Tales Paris. *Carolyn revised* the Boston, North Shore, Pioneer Valley, and Berkshires *sections of the* Massachusetts *chapter.*

Maine revisor **Hilary Nangle** *lives in Waldoboro, Maine. She is features editor for the* Times Record, *a daily newspaper in Brunswick, for which she works on the travel and arts and entertainment pages. She also freelances regularly for travel and ski magazines.*

Vermont updater **Anne Peracca** *grew up in Connecticut but was drawn to Vermont for its skiing. Anne, who is earning a degree in natural resources planning, likes to be out and about—whether it's to visit B&Bs or to hit the slopes.*

Alan W. Petrucelli's *work has appeared in such publications as the* New York Times, Redbook, People, Ladies' Home Journal, USA Weekend, McCall's, Family Circle, *and the* Cape Cod Times. *He put his journalistic skills to work on southeastern Massachusetts—the area he calls home—and the mid- and upper sections of the Cape.*

Our Rhode Island correspondent, **K. D. Weaver,** *is the editor of the* Block Island Times *newspaper and a stringer for the Associated Press. He is a 1995 graduate of Columbia's Graduate School of Journalism.*

Contents

Foreword

Although every care has been taken to ensure the accuracy of the information in this guide, the passage of time will always bring change, and, consequently, the publisher cannot accept responsibility for errors that may occur.

All prices and listings are based on information available to us at press time. Details may change, however, and the prudent traveler will avoid inconvenience by calling ahead.

Fodor's wants to hear about your travel experiences, both pleasant and unpleasant. When an inn or B&B fails to live up to its billing, let us know and we will investigate the complaint and revise our entries where the facts warrant it.

Send your letters to the editors of Fodor's Travel Publications, 201 East 50th Street, New York, NY 10022.

Introduction

You'll find bed-and-breakfasts in big houses with turrets and little houses with decks, in mansions by the water and cabins in the forest, not to mention in structures of many sizes and shapes in between. B&Bs are run by people who were once lawyers and writers, homemakers and artists, nurses and architects, singers and businesspeople. Some B&Bs are just a room or two in a hospitable local's home; others are more like small inns. So every B&B stay has a quality of serendipity.

But while that's part of the pleasure of the experience, it's also an excellent reason to plan your B&B travels with a good B&B guide. The one you hold in your hands serves the purpose neatly.

To create it, we've hand-picked a team of professional writers who are also confirmed B&B lovers: people who adore the many manifestations of the Victorian era; who go wild over wicker and brass beds, four-posters and fireplaces; and who know a well-run operation when they see it and are only too eager to communicate their knowledge to you. We've instructed them to inspect the premises and check out every corner of the premier B&Bs and inns in the areas they cover and to report critically on only the best in every price range.

They've returned from their travels with comprehensive reports on the very best B&Bs—establishments that promise a unique experience, a distinctive sense of time and space. All are destinations in themselves, not just places to rest your head at night but an integral part of a weekend escape. You'll learn what's good, what's bad, and what could be better; what our writers liked and what you might not like.

At the same time, Fodor's reviewers tell you what's up in the area and what you should and shouldn't miss—everything from historic sites and parks to antiques shops, boutiques, and the area's niftiest restaurants and nightspots. We also include names and addresses of B&B reservations services, just in case you're inspired to seek out additional properties on your own. Reviews are organized by region.

In the italicized service information that starts and ends every review, a second address in parentheses is a mailing address. A double room (called just "double" throughout) is for two people, regardless of the size or type of beds. Rates are for two, excluding tax, in the high season; details about meals and extras that are included follow the rates (be sure to ask about special packages and midweek or off-season discounts). Unless otherwise stated, rooms don't have phones or TVs. Regarding bathrooms: Note that even the most stunning homes, farmhouses and mansions alike, may not provide a private bathroom for each room.

What we call a restaurant serves meals other than breakfast and is usually open to the general public. At inns listed as operating on the Modified American Plan (MAP), rates include two meals, generally breakfast and dinner.

Where applicable, we note seasonal and other restrictions. Although we abhor discrimination, we have conveyed information about innkeepers' restrictive practices so that you will be aware of the prevailing attitudes. Such discriminatory practices are most often applied to parents traveling with small children, who may not—in any case—feel comfortable having their offspring toddle amid breakable bric-a-brac and near precipitous stairways.

The following credit-card abbreviations are used throughout this guide: AE, American Express; D, Discover; DC, Diners Club; MC, MasterCard; V, Visa.

When traveling the B&B way, always call ahead; and if you have mobility problems or are traveling with children, if you prefer a private bath or a certain type of bed, or if you have specific dietary needs or any other concerns, discuss them with the innkeeper. At the same time, if you're traveling to an inn because of a specific feature, make sure that it will be available when you get there and not closed for renovation. The same goes if you're making a detour to take advantage of specific sights or attractions.

It's a sad commentary on other B&B guides today that we feel obliged to tell you that our writers did, in fact, visit every property in person and that it is they, not the innkeepers, who wrote the reviews. No one paid a fee or promised to sell or promote the book in order to be included in it. (In fact, one of the most challenging parts of the work of Fodor's writers is to persuade innkeepers and B&B owners that he or she wants nothing more than a tour of the premises and answers to a few questions!) Fodor's has no stake in anything but the truth. If a room is dark, with peeling wallpaper, we don't call it quaint or atmospheric—we call it run-down and then steer you to a more appealing section of the property.

So trust us, the way you'd trust a knowledgeable, well-traveled friend. Let us hear from you about your travels, whether you found that the B&Bs you visited surpassed their descriptions or the other way around. And have a wonderful trip!

Karen Cure
Editorial Director

New England

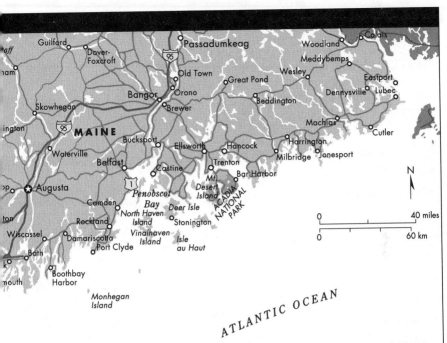

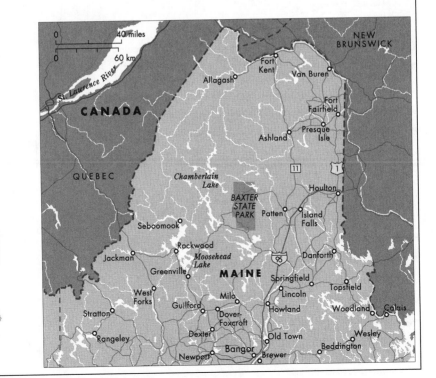

Special Features at a Glance

Name of Property	Accessible for People with Disabilities	Antiques	On the Water	Good Value	Car Not Necessary	Full Meal Service	Historic Building	Romantic Hideaway
CONNECTICUT								
Antiques & Accommodations		✓					✓	✓
The Barney House		✓		✓			✓	✓
Bee & Thistle Inn		✓	✓	✓		✓	✓	✓
Bishopsgate Inn		✓		✓		✓	✓	✓
The Boulders		✓	✓			✓	✓	✓
Captain Stannard House		✓		✓	✓		✓	
Chimney Crest Manor		✓		✓			✓	✓
Copper Beech Inn	✓	✓				✓	✓	✓
The Cotswold Inn					✓			✓
The Country Goose		✓		✓			✓	✓
The Curtis House	✓			✓		✓	✓	
The Elms Inn	✓	✓		✓	✓	✓	✓	
Greenwoods Gate		✓					✓	✓
Griswold Inn		✓				✓	✓	
Harbor House Inn				✓			✓	
Harbour Inne & Cottage			✓	✓	✓			
The Homestead Inn (Greenwich)		✓				✓	✓	✓
The Homestead Inn (New Milford)		✓		✓			✓	
Hopkins Inn			✓	✓		✓	✓	✓
House on the Hill		✓		✓			✓	✓
The Inn at National Hall		✓	✓	✓		✓	✓	✓
Lasbury's Guest House			✓	✓	✓		✓	
Manor House		✓		✓			✓	✓
The Maples Inn		✓					✓	✓

	Luxurious	Pets Allowed	No Smoking Indoors	Good Place for Families	Near Arts Festivals	Beach Nearby	Cross-Country Ski Trail	Golf within 5 Miles	Fitness Facilities	Good Biking Terrain	Skiing	Horseback Riding	Tennis	Swimming on Premises	Hiking Nearby
	✓	✓	✓		✓	✓		✓		✓		✓			✓
			✓	✓			✓	✓		✓	✓		✓		✓
	✓		✓		✓	✓		✓		✓					✓
			✓					✓		✓			✓		✓
	✓		✓		✓	✓	✓	✓		✓	✓	✓	✓	✓	✓
			✓			✓		✓		✓			✓	✓	
	✓		✓			✓	✓	✓				✓		✓	✓
	✓							✓		✓					✓
	✓					✓	✓	✓		✓					
			✓		✓		✓	✓			✓				✓
				✓	✓			✓	✓	✓	✓		✓		✓
			✓	✓	✓			✓		✓		✓	✓		✓
	✓		✓		✓	✓	✓	✓		✓	✓	✓	✓		✓
			✓	✓	✓	✓		✓		✓					✓
			✓		✓	✓		✓		✓			✓	✓	✓
		✓			✓	✓	✓	✓		✓			✓		✓
	✓							✓					✓		✓
					✓	✓		✓				✓			✓
					✓	✓	✓	✓		✓	✓			✓	✓
	✓	✓	✓	✓			✓	✓				✓	✓	✓	
	✓		✓		✓	✓		✓		✓					
			✓	✓	✓	✓		✓		✓	✓		✓	✓	✓
	✓		✓		✓	✓	✓	✓		✓	✓	✓	✓	✓	✓
	✓		✓	✓	✓			✓		✓	✓			✓	✓

Special Features at a Glance

Name of Property	Accessible for People with Disabilities	Antiques	On the Water	Good Value	Car Not Necessary	Full Meal Service	Historic Building	Romantic Hideaway
The Mayflower Inn	✓	✓				✓		✓
Old Lyme Inn	✓	✓				✓	✓	
Old Riverton Inn			✓			✓	✓	
The Palmer Inn		✓					✓	✓
Randall's Ordinary		✓				✓	✓	✓
Riverwind		✓		✓			✓	✓
Roger Sherman Inn						✓	✓	
Silvermine Tavern		✓	✓	✓		✓	✓	✓
Simsbury 1820 House	✓	✓		✓		✓	✓	✓
The Stanton House Inn				✓			✓	
Steamboat Inn	✓		✓		✓		✓	✓
Stonecroft	✓						✓	✓
Stonehenge	✓		✓			✓		✓
Talcott House		✓	✓					✓
Three Chimneys Inn	✓	✓		✓	✓		✓	✓
Tidewater Inn		✓					✓	✓
Tollgate Hill Inn & Restaurant	✓	✓				✓	✓	✓
Tucker Hill Inn				✓				
Under Mountain Inn		✓		✓		✓	✓	✓
West Lane Inn	✓	✓					✓	
The White Hart	✓					✓	✓	✓
MAINE								
The Admiral Perry House		✓					✓	
Augustus Bove House		✓	✓	✓			✓	
Bear Mountain Inn			✓	✓				

Luxurious	Pets Allowed	No Smoking Indoors	Good Place for Families	Near Arts Festivals	Beach Nearby	Cross-Country Ski Trail	Golf within 5 Miles	Fitness Facilities	Good Biking Terrain	Skiing	Horseback Riding	Tennis	Swimming on Premises	Hiking Nearby
✓		✓		✓		✓	✓	✓		✓		✓	✓	✓
✓	✓		✓	✓	✓		✓		✓					✓
	✓			✓	✓	✓	✓		✓	✓				✓
		✓		✓	✓		✓		✓			✓		
			✓		✓		✓		✓					✓
✓							✓		✓			✓		✓
		✓		✓			✓		✓		✓	✓		✓
			✓	✓	✓		✓		✓					✓
	✓		✓	✓		✓	✓		✓	✓				✓
		✓			✓		✓						✓	
✓		✓		✓	✓		✓		✓					✓
✓		✓		✓	✓	✓	✓		✓		✓	✓		✓
✓						✓			✓		✓	✓		✓
		✓			✓		✓		✓		✓			
✓		✓		✓	✓		✓	✓						
		✓		✓	✓				✓					✓
✓	✓					✓	✓		✓	✓	✓	✓		✓
		✓			✓	✓	✓		✓	✓	✓	✓	✓	✓
		✓	✓	✓	✓	✓	✓		✓	✓	✓	✓	✓	✓
			✓	✓			✓		✓			✓	✓	
	✓		✓	✓	✓	✓	✓		✓	✓	✓			✓
		✓		✓	✓				✓				✓	✓
	✓	✓	✓	✓	✓		✓		✓	✓			✓	✓
		✓	✓	✓		✓	✓		✓	✓			✓	✓

Special Features at a Glance

Name of Property	Accessible for People with Disabilities	Antiques	On the Water	Good Value	Car Not Necessary	Full Meal Service	Historic Building	Romantic Hideaway
Black Point Inn	✓	✓	✓		✓	✓		✓
Blue Hill Inn		✓				✓		
Brewer House		✓	✓				✓	
The Briar Rose		✓		✓				
The Bridgton House		✓						
Buck's Harbor Inn				✓				
Bufflehead Cove			✓	✓				✓
The Camden Maine Stay		✓		✓			✓	
The Captain Lord Mansion		✓					✓	✓
The Captain's Hideaway								✓
The Castine Inn						✓	✓	
Chesuncook Lake House			✓		✓	✓	✓	
Claremont Hotel			✓	✓		✓	✓	✓
The Crocker House Inn				✓		✓		
The East Wind Inn & Meeting House			✓	✓		✓		
Edgecomb-Coles House		✓						✓
Edward's Harborside Inn		✓	✓					✓
Eggemoggin Beach Bed and Breakfast		✓	✓					✓
Five Gables Inn			✓				✓	✓
The Flying Cloud		✓	✓					
Goose Cove Lodge		✓	✓			✓		✓
Grant's Kennebago Camps			✓		✓	✓		
Greenville Inn		✓					✓	
Homeport Inn		✓	✓	✓			✓	✓
Inn at Bay Lodge		✓	✓					✓
Inn at Canoe Point		✓	✓					✓

Luxurious	Pets Allowed	No Smoking Indoors	Good Place for Families	Near Arts Festivals	Beach Nearby	Cross-Country Ski Trail	Golf within 5 Miles	Fitness Facilities	Good Biking Terrain	Skiing	Horseback Riding	Tennis	Swimming on Premises	Hiking Nearby
✓		✓	✓		✓		✓	✓	✓			✓	✓	
		✓							✓					
		✓												
		✓			✓		✓		✓					✓
			✓	✓	✓		✓		✓					✓
	✓	✓	✓						✓					
✓		✓		✓	✓	✓	✓		✓					
		✓			✓	✓	✓		✓	✓				✓
✓		✓			✓		✓		✓					
✓		✓			✓		✓		✓					
					✓		✓		✓					
	✓	✓	✓										✓	✓
			✓	✓	✓		✓		✓			✓		✓
	✓								✓					
	✓								✓					✓
✓		✓			✓	✓	✓		✓	✓				✓
		✓	✓				✓		✓					
✓		✓							✓					
		✓			✓		✓		✓					
		✓	✓						✓					
		✓	✓		✓		✓		✓				✓	✓
			✓		✓				✓				✓	✓
		✓					✓		✓	✓				✓
✓									✓					
✓		✓			✓		✓	✓	✓				✓	✓
✓		✓		✓	✓		✓		✓				✓	✓

Special Features at a Glance

Name of Property	Accessible for People with Disabilities	Antiques	On the Water	Good Value	Car Not Necessary	Full Meal Service	Historic Building	Romantic Hideaway
Inn at the River	✓		✓					
Inn on the Harbor	✓		✓					
The Isaac Randall House		✓						✓
The Island House		✓		✓			✓	
Island View Inn		✓	✓					✓
The John Peters Inn		✓	✓				✓	✓
The Keeper's House		✓	✓		✓	✓	✓	✓
Lake House								✓
Le Domaine						✓		✓
The Lodge at Moosehead Lake								✓
The Maine Stay Inn and Cottages							✓	
The Marston House				✓				
Mill Pond Inn			✓	✓				✓
Mira Monte								
The Newcastle Inn		✓	✓			✓		✓
The Noble House			✓					✓
Oceanside Meadows	✓	✓	✓					
The Oxford House						✓		
Peacock House	✓							
Pilgrim's Inn		✓	✓			✓	✓	✓
Pleasant Bay Inn and Llama Keep		✓	✓	✓				
Popham Beach Bed & Breakfast			✓				✓	✓
Quisiana			✓			✓		
Riverbank on the Harbor		✓	✓					✓
Rockmere Lodge		✓	✓					✓
The 1774 Inn		✓	✓	✓			✓	

Luxurious	Pets Allowed	No Smoking Indoors	Good Place for Families	Near Arts Festivals	Beach Nearby	Cross-Country Ski Trail	Golf within 5 Miles	Fitness Facilities	Good Biking Terrain	Skiing	Horseback Riding	Tennis	Swimming on Premises	Hiking Nearby
			✓											
		✓	✓				✓		✓					
✓		✓	✓				✓							
		✓		✓			✓		✓					✓
		✓			✓				✓				✓	✓
✓		✓							✓					
		✓							✓					
		✓			✓		✓							✓
														✓
✓		✓							✓					✓
		✓		✓			✓		✓					
		✓							✓					
									✓				✓	
				✓	✓		✓		✓					✓
		✓							✓					
							✓			✓				✓
	✓	✓	✓		✓				✓				✓	✓
		✓	✓	✓	✓				✓	✓				✓
									✓					✓
✓				✓	✓				✓					
		✓							✓					
		✓			✓		✓		✓				✓	
			✓									✓	✓	✓
		✓					✓		✓					
		✓	✓				✓		✓					
		✓			✓		✓		✓				✓	

Special Features at a Glance

Name of Property	Accessible for People with Disabilities	Antiques	On the Water	Good Value	Car Not Necessary	Full Meal Service	Historic Building	Romantic Hideaway
Sky Lodge						✓	✓	
The Squire Tarbox Inn		✓				✓		✓
The Tides		✓	✓				✓	✓
Ullikana		✓					✓	✓
Victorian Inn		✓						
The Waterford Inne		✓		✓		✓		
The Weston House		✓		✓			✓	
Whitehall Inn		✓				✓	✓	
York Harbor Inn		✓				✓	✓	✓
The Youngtown Inn								
MASSACHUSETTS								
Addison Choate Inn	✓	✓		✓	✓		✓	
Admiral Benbow Inn		✓			✓		✓	
The Allen House	✓	✓		✓			✓	
Amelia Payson Guest House	✓			✓	✓			
Apple Tree Inn		✓				✓	✓	✓
Ashley Manor		✓					✓	✓
Augustus Snow House		✓				✓	✓	✓
Bay Beach			✓					✓
The Bayberry		✓						
Beach House Inn			✓	✓				✓
Beach Plum Inn and Cottages						✓		✓
Beacon Hill Bed and Breakfast		✓			✓		✓	
Beechwood		✓					✓	✓
The Bertram Inn	✓	✓		✓	✓			

Luxurious	Pets Allowed	No Smoking Indoors	Good Place for Families	Near Arts Festivals	Beach Nearby	Cross-Country Ski Trail	Golf within 5 Miles	Fitness Facilities	Good Biking Terrain	Skiing	Horseback Riding	Tennis	Swimming on Premises	Hiking Nearby
			✓				✓							
✓		✓				✓			✓					
✓		✓		✓	✓		✓		✓					✓
✓		✓		✓	✓		✓		✓					✓
		✓	✓	✓			✓							✓
	✓	✓			✓	✓			✓	✓				✓
		✓							✓					✓
					✓		✓		✓					
		✓			✓		✓		✓					✓
		✓			✓				✓					✓
✓		✓			✓								✓	
		✓	✓		✓		✓		✓					✓
✓		✓												
		✓			✓									
✓		✓		✓	✓	✓	✓		✓	✓	✓	✓	✓	✓
		✓			✓		✓		✓			✓		
✓					✓		✓		✓					✓
✓		✓			✓		✓	✓	✓				✓	✓
		✓			✓		✓		✓					✓
		✓	✓		✓									
		✓	✓		✓				✓			✓		✓
		✓												
		✓			✓		✓		✓					✓
	✓	✓												

Special Features at a Glance

Name of Property	Accessible for People with Disabilities	Antiques	On the Water	Good Value	Car Not Necessary	Full Meal Service	Historic Building	Romantic Hideaway
Blantyre	✓	✓					✓	✓
Brandt House		✓						✓
The Brass Key		✓			✓		✓	✓
Brewster Farmhouse		✓					✓	✓
Brook Farm Inn	✓	✓		✓				✓
A Cambridge House Bed-and-Breakfast	✓	✓			✓			
The Candlelight Inn		✓				✓	✓	✓
The Captain Farris House		✓		✓				✓
Captain Freeman Inn		✓		✓	✓		✓	
Captain's House Inn		✓					✓	✓
Centerboard Guest House		✓			✓		✓	✓
Century House					✓		✓	
Charlotte Inn		✓			✓	✓	✓	✓
Chatham Bars Inn	✓		✓	✓		✓	✓	✓
Clark Currier Inn	✓	✓		✓	✓		✓	✓
Clark Tavern Inn		✓		✓			✓	✓
Cliff Lodge		✓			✓		✓	
Cliffwood Inn		✓					✓	✓
Corner House		✓		✓	✓		✓	✓
Crocker House Inn		✓		✓	✓			✓
The Daggett House		✓	✓		✓		✓	✓
Dalton House	✓			✓				
Deerfield Inn	✓	✓				✓	✓	✓
Duck Inn		✓		✓			✓	✓
Eden Pines Inn			✓					✓
Edgewater Bed and Breakfast		✓	✓				✓	✓

Luxurious	Pets Allowed	No Smoking Indoors	Good Place for Families	Near Arts Festivals	Beach Nearby	Cross-Country Ski Trail	Golf within 5 Miles	Fitness Facilities	Good Biking Terrain	Skiing	Horseback Riding	Tennis	Swimming on Premises	Hiking Nearby
✓				✓		✓	✓	✓	✓	✓	✓	✓	✓	✓
	✓	✓	✓		✓	✓		✓				✓		✓
✓				✓	✓	✓		✓						✓
✓		✓			✓		✓		✓				✓	
		✓		✓		✓	✓		✓	✓	✓		✓	✓
		✓												
				✓		✓	✓		✓	✓	✓			✓
✓		✓			✓		✓							
		✓			✓	✓	✓	✓	✓				✓	✓
✓		✓		✓	✓		✓		✓					✓
✓					✓		✓		✓					✓
		✓	✓		✓		✓		✓					✓
✓					✓		✓		✓					✓
✓			✓	✓	✓		✓	✓	✓			✓	✓	✓
✓		✓			✓						✓			
		✓											✓	
					✓				✓					✓
✓		✓		✓			✓		✓	✓	✓		✓	✓
					✓		✓		✓					✓
		✓			✓				✓					
		✓	✓		✓	✓			✓					✓
		✓	✓	✓		✓			✓	✓	✓		✓	✓
✓		✓	✓	✓		✓			✓					✓
	✓	✓	✓		✓				✓					✓
		✓			✓									

Special Features at a Glance

Name of Property	Accessible for People with Disabilities	Antiques	On the Water	Good Value	Car Not Necessary	Full Meal Service	Historic Building	Romantic Hideaway
82 Chandler Street				✓	✓			
Field Farm	✓			✓			✓	✓
The Four Chimneys Inn		✓					✓	✓
Foxglove Cottage		✓		✓			✓	
The Gables Inn		✓					✓	✓
Garrison Inn	✓	✓			✓	✓	✓	
Gateways Inn		✓				✓	✓	✓
Greenwood House								
Harbor Light Inn		✓			✓		✓	✓
Harborside House			✓		✓			✓
Heaven on High		✓						✓
The Inn at Fernbrook		✓					✓	✓
Inn at Sandwich Center		✓		✓			✓	✓
Inn on Cove Hill	✓	✓		✓	✓		✓	
Inn on the Sound			✓	✓				✓
Isaiah Clark House		✓		✓	✓	✓	✓	
Isaiah Hall B&B Inn		✓		✓			✓	
Isaiah Jones Homestead		✓		✓			✓	✓
Ivanhoe Country House	✓	✓		✓				
Jackson-Russell-Whitfield House		✓					✓	
Jared Coffin House	✓	✓			✓	✓	✓	
The John Jeffries House	✓				✓			
Lambert's Cove Country Inn				✓		✓	✓	✓
The Little Red House				✓				
Lizzie Borden Bed and Breakfast		✓			✓		✓	
Lord Jeffery Inn	✓	✓			✓	✓		

Luxurious	Pets Allowed	No Smoking Indoors	Good Place for Families	Near Arts Festivals	Beach Nearby	Cross-Country Ski Trail	Golf within 5 Miles	Fitness Facilities	Good Biking Terrain	Skiing	Horseback Riding	Tennis	Swimming on Premises	Hiking Nearby
		✓												
✓		✓	✓			✓			✓	✓		✓	✓	✓
		✓		✓	✓				✓					✓
		✓												
✓				✓		✓	✓		✓	✓	✓	✓	✓	✓
			✓		✓						✓			
✓		✓		✓		✓	✓		✓	✓	✓			✓
		✓			✓				✓					
✓					✓								✓	
		✓			✓									
✓		✓			✓									
		✓			✓		✓		✓					✓
		✓			✓				✓					✓
		✓			✓									
		✓			✓									
		✓	✓		✓		✓		✓					
					✓		✓		✓					
✓		✓			✓		✓		✓					✓
	✓					✓	✓		✓	✓			✓	✓
		✓			✓									
	✓				✓		✓		✓					✓
			✓											
					✓				✓			✓	✓	✓
		✓												
		✓												
	✓		✓			✓			✓					

Special Features at a Glance

Name of Property	Accessible for People with Disabilities	Antiques	On the Water	Good Value	Car Not Necessary	Full Meal Service	Historic Building	Romantic Hideaway	
Martin House Inn		✓			✓		✓	✓	
The Mary Prentiss Inn		✓			✓		✓	✓	
Merrell Tavern Inn	✓	✓		✓			✓	✓	
Miles River Country Inn		✓					✓	✓	
Moses Nickerson House		✓					✓	✓	
Mostly Hall		✓		✓	✓		✓	✓	
New Boston Inn	✓	✓				✓	✓	✓	
Newbury Guest House	✓				✓				
Northfield Country House		✓		✓				✓	
Oak House		✓	✓		✓		✓	✓	
Onset Pointe Inn		✓	✓	✓			✓	✓	
The Orchards	✓	✓				✓		✓	
Outermost Inn			✓			✓		✓	
Penny House Inn		✓		✓			✓		
The Publick House & Colonel Ebenezer Crafts Inn	✓	✓				✓	✓		
The Red Lion Inn	✓	✓				✓	✓		
River Bend Farm		✓		✓			✓	✓	
Rookwood Inn		✓					✓	✓	
The Ruddy Turnstone		✓		✓			✓	✓	
Sally Webster Inn		✓		✓	✓		✓	✓	
Salt Marsh Farm		✓		✓			✓	✓	
The Saltworks		✓		✓			✓	✓	
Sconehedge		✓					✓	✓	
Seacrest Manor		✓						✓	
Sea Spray Inn		✓		✓	✓		✓	✓	
Seaward Inn	✓	✓	✓			✓			

Luxurious	Pets Allowed	No Smoking Indoors	Good Place for Families	Near Arts Festivals	Beach Nearby	Cross-Country Ski Trail	Golf within 5 Miles	Fitness Facilities	Good Biking Terrain	Skiing	Horseback Riding	Tennis	Swimming on Premises	Hiking Nearby
					✓		✓		✓					✓
		✓												
✓		✓		✓		✓	✓		✓	✓	✓			✓
	✓	✓	✓		✓	✓	✓		✓			✓		
		✓		✓		✓			✓					✓
✓		✓			✓		✓		✓					✓
	✓	✓	✓			✓			✓		✓			✓
						✓			✓			✓	✓	✓
✓					✓		✓		✓					✓
✓		✓	✓		✓				✓				✓	
✓		✓	✓			✓		✓	✓	✓			✓	✓
					✓				✓					
		✓	✓	✓	✓	✓	✓		✓					✓
	✓		✓			✓		✓				✓	✓	✓
			✓	✓		✓	✓	✓	✓	✓	✓		✓	✓
		✓	✓			✓			✓	✓	✓		✓	✓
✓		✓	✓	✓		✓	✓		✓	✓	✓			✓
		✓		✓	✓	✓			✓					✓
		✓			✓									
			✓		✓		✓		✓					✓
		✓			✓				✓					
✓		✓												
		✓			✓				✓					
		✓			✓		✓		✓				✓	✓
			✓		✓				✓					

Special Features at a Glance

Name of Property	Accessible for People with Disabilities	Antiques	On the Water	Good Value	Car Not Necessary	Full Meal Service	Historic Building	Romantic Hideaway
Seven Sea Street					✓			
76 Main Street	✓	✓			✓		✓	
Shiverick Inn		✓			✓		✓	✓
South Hollow Vineyards Inn		✓		✓			✓	✓
Sturbridge Country Inn	✓	✓						✓
Summer House		✓	✓		✓	✓	✓	✓
Sunnyside Farm Bed and Breakfast		✓		✓				
Ten Lyon Street Inn		✓			✓			✓
Thorncroft Inn	✓	✓					✓	✓
The Tuck Inn		✓		✓	✓		✓	✓
The Turning Point Inn		✓					✓	
Victorian Inn		✓			✓		✓	✓
Village Green Inn		✓		✓	✓		✓	✓
The Wauwinet	✓	✓	✓		✓	✓	✓	✓
The Weathervane Inn	✓							
Wedgewood Inn		✓		✓			✓	✓
Westmoor Inn		✓			✓		✓	✓
Wheatleigh	✓	✓				✓	✓	✓
Whistler's Inn	✓	✓					✓	✓
White Elephant	✓	✓	✓		✓	✓	✓	
Wildflower Inn		✓		✓	✓			✓
The Williamsville Inn	✓	✓				✓	✓	✓
Windflower Inn	✓	✓					✓	✓
The Windsor House		✓				✓	✓	
Wingscorton Farm		✓		✓			✓	✓
Wood Duck Inn		✓		✓				✓

Luxurious	Pets Allowed	No Smoking Indoors	Good Place for Families	Near Arts Festivals	Beach Nearby	Cross-Country Ski Trail	Golf within 5 Miles	Fitness Facilities	Good Biking Terrain	Skiing	Horseback Riding	Tennis	Swimming on Premises	Hiking Nearby
		✓			✓		✓		✓					
		✓	✓		✓		✓		✓					✓
✓		✓			✓		✓		✓					
		✓		✓	✓	✓	✓		✓					✓
						✓			✓					✓
			✓		✓		✓		✓			✓	✓	✓
		✓				✓			✓				✓	✓
		✓			✓		✓		✓					
✓		✓			✓		✓		✓					✓
		✓	✓		✓								✓	
		✓	✓	✓		✓	✓		✓	✓	✓			✓
	✓	✓			✓		✓		✓					✓
		✓			✓				✓					✓
✓		✓	✓		✓		✓		✓			✓	✓	✓
		✓		✓		✓	✓		✓	✓	✓		✓	✓
✓		✓			✓		✓		✓					
		✓			✓				✓					
✓				✓		✓	✓	✓	✓	✓	✓	✓	✓	✓
✓		✓	✓	✓		✓	✓		✓	✓	✓			✓
			✓		✓		✓		✓				✓	✓
		✓			✓				✓					
		✓				✓			✓	✓		✓	✓	✓
			✓	✓		✓	✓		✓	✓	✓		✓	✓
			✓	✓	✓		✓		✓					✓
	✓		✓		✓						✓			✓
									✓					✓

Special Features at a Glance

Name of Property	Accessible for People with Disabilities	Antiques	On the Water	Good Value	Car Not Necessary	Full Meal Service	Historic Building	Romantic Hideaway
Yankee Clipper Inn	✓	✓	✓			✓	✓	✓
Yankee Pedlar Inn	✓	✓		✓		✓		
NEW HAMPSHIRE								
Adair Lodge		✓					✓	✓
Amos A. Parker House		✓					✓	✓
The Benjamin Prescott Inn		✓					✓	
The Birchwood Inn		✓					✓	
The Blanchard House		✓					✓	
Candlelite Inn		✓					✓	
The Chase House		✓					✓	✓
Colby Hill Inn		✓				✓	✓	
The Covered Bridge House				✓				
Exeter Inn	✓	✓				✓		
Ferry Point House		✓	✓	✓			✓	✓
Foxglove, A Country Inn		✓						✓
The Franconia Inn		✓				✓		✓
The Governor's Inn				✓		✓	✓	
The Hancock Inn		✓					✓	✓
Hannah Davis House		✓					✓	✓
Highland Farm Bed and Breakfast		✓					✓	
Home Hill Country Inn & French Restaurant		✓				✓		✓
The Horse & Hound Inn		✓				✓		✓
Inn at Christian Shore		✓		✓	✓		✓	
Inn at Crystal Lake		✓						✓
Inn at Maplewood Farm		✓					✓	✓

Luxurious	Pets Allowed	No Smoking Indoors	Good Place for Families	Near Arts Festivals	Beach Nearby	Cross-Country Ski Trail	Golf within 5 Miles	Fitness Facilities	Good Biking Terrain	Skiing	Horseback Riding	Tennis	Swimming on Premises	Hiking Nearby
✓		✓	✓		✓				✓				✓	
			✓							✓				
✓		✓							✓	✓			✓	✓
		✓		✓		✓			✓					✓
		✓	✓			✓			✓					✓
		✓	✓						✓					✓
		✓			✓				✓					✓
		✓	✓	✓	✓				✓					✓
		✓						✓	✓				✓	
		✓	✓			✓			✓	✓		✓	✓	✓
					✓	✓	✓		✓	✓			✓	✓
	✓		✓	✓				✓	✓					
		✓	✓						✓					
		✓					✓			✓				✓
		✓	✓			✓	✓		✓	✓	✓	✓	✓	✓
		✓					✓					✓		
		✓			✓				✓	✓				✓
		✓		✓		✓			✓					✓
		✓		✓		✓			✓					✓
			✓			✓	✓		✓			✓	✓	✓
		✓				✓	✓		✓	✓				✓
		✓		✓			✓							
		✓	✓		✓	✓	✓		✓	✓				
		✓					✓		✓	✓				✓

Special Features at a Glance

Name of Property	Accessible for People with Disabilities	Antiques	On the Water	Good Value	Car Not Necessary	Full Meal Service	Historic Building	Romantic Hideaway	
Inn at Thorn Hill		✓				✓	✓	✓	
The Inn on Golden Pond		✓						✓	
The Inn on Newfound Lake		✓	✓			✓		✓	
The Lavender Flower Inn		✓							
Manor on Golden Pond		✓	✓			✓	✓	✓	
Martin Hill Inn		✓			✓		✓	✓	
The Mary Chase Inn		✓					✓		
Moody Parsonage Bed and Breakfast	✓	✓		✓			✓		
The Mulburn Inn		✓					✓		
Notchland Inn		✓				✓	✓	✓	
The Nutmeg Inn		✓					✓	✓	
The Oceanside		✓	✓						
Red Hill Inn		✓				✓		✓	
Rock Ledge Manor		✓	✓	✓					
Rosewood Country Inn		✓						✓	
The 1785 Inn		✓				✓	✓	✓	
Sise Inn	✓	✓			✓		✓	✓	
Snowvillage Inn		✓				✓	✓	✓	
Sugar Hill Inn		✓				✓			
Sunset Hill House		✓				✓	✓	✓	
The Tamworth Inn		✓				✓	✓	✓	
The Victoria Inn		✓				✓	✓		
The Wakefield Inn		✓		✓			✓	✓	
Whitneys' Inn		✓				✓	✓		
The Wolfeboro Inn	✓	✓	✓		✓	✓	✓	✓	
Zahn's Alpine Guest House				✓					

	Luxurious	Pets Allowed	No Smoking Indoors	Good Place for Families	Near Arts Festivals	Beach Nearby	Cross-Country Ski Trail	Golf within 5 Miles	Fitness Facilities	Good Biking Terrain	Skiing	Horseback Riding	Tennis	Swimming on Premises	Hiking Nearby
	✓		✓		✓		✓			✓	✓			✓	✓
			✓		✓	✓	✓			✓					✓
				✓		✓	✓			✓	✓				✓
			✓	✓			✓	✓		✓	✓				✓
	✓		✓				✓			✓			✓	✓	✓
			✓		✓										
			✓												✓
			✓	✓	✓			✓	✓	✓					
			✓	✓	✓		✓	✓		✓	✓				✓
	✓		✓					✓			✓			✓	✓
			✓	✓	✓	✓	✓	✓		✓				✓	
	✓		✓	✓	✓	✓		✓		✓					
					✓	✓	✓	✓		✓			✓		✓
			✓		✓	✓		✓		✓					✓
			✓		✓	✓				✓	✓				✓
			✓	✓	✓		✓	✓		✓	✓		✓	✓	✓
	✓				✓			✓							
			✓	✓		✓	✓	✓			✓		✓		✓
			✓	✓	✓		✓	✓		✓	✓				✓
			✓				✓	✓			✓			✓	✓
			✓	✓						✓				✓	✓
			✓		✓	✓		✓		✓					
				✓						✓					
		✓		✓	✓		✓	✓		✓	✓			✓	✓
	✓			✓	✓	✓	✓	✓		✓			✓	✓	
			✓							✓					

Special Features at a Glance

Name of Property	Accessible for People with Disabilities	Antiques	On the Water	Good Value	Car Not Necessary	Full Meal Service	Historic Building	Romantic Hideaway	
RHODE ISLAND									
Admiral Dewey Inn		✓	✓				✓	✓	
Admiral Fitzroy Inn	✓	✓			✓		✓	✓	
Atlantic Inn		✓			✓		✓	✓	
Barrington Inn		✓			✓		✓		
Blue Dory Inn		✓	✓	✓	✓		✓	✓	
Cliffside Inn		✓					✓	✓	
Elm Tree Cottage		✓					✓	✓	
Francis Malbone House	✓	✓			✓		✓	✓	
Hotel Manisses		✓			✓	✓	✓	✓	
The Inn at Castle Hill		✓	✓			✓	✓	✓	
The Inntowne	✓	✓			✓				
Ivy Lodge		✓		✓			✓	✓	
Ocean House		✓	✓		✓	✓	✓		
The Richards		✓		✓			✓		
Rose Farm Inn		✓			✓		✓	✓	
Sanford-Covell Villa Marina		✓	✓	✓	✓		✓	✓	
Shelter Harbor Inn		✓				✓	✓	✓	
The 1661 Inn & Guest House		✓	✓		✓		✓	✓	
Stone Lea		✓	✓				✓	✓	
Surf Hotel		✓	✓	✓	✓		✓		
Victorian Ladies		✓					✓	✓	
Weekapaug Inn	✓	✓	✓			✓	✓		

Luxurious	Pets Allowed	No Smoking Indoors	Good Place for Families	Near Arts Festivals	Beach Nearby	Cross-Country Ski Trail	Golf within 5 Miles	Fitness Facilities	Good Biking Terrain	Skiing	Horseback Riding	Tennis	Swimming on Premises	Hiking Nearby
		✓	✓		✓				✓					✓
			✓	✓	✓									
✓		✓	✓		✓				✓			✓		✓
		✓			✓				✓					✓
✓		✓			✓				✓					✓
✓		✓		✓	✓									✓
✓		✓		✓	✓				✓					✓
✓		✓		✓	✓									
✓					✓				✓					✓
				✓	✓	✓			✓					✓
			✓	✓	✓			✓						
✓		✓	✓	✓	✓									
			✓	✓	✓		✓		✓					✓
		✓			✓				✓					✓
		✓		✓	✓				✓					✓
✓				✓	✓								✓	
✓			✓	✓	✓		✓	✓	✓			✓		✓
✓				✓	✓				✓					✓
✓		✓			✓				✓					✓
			✓	✓	✓				✓					✓
		✓		✓	✓				✓					✓
			✓	✓	✓		✓		✓			✓		✓

Special Features at a Glance

Name of Property	Accessible for People with Disabilities	Antiques	On the Water	Good Value	Car Not Necessary	Full Meal Service	Historic Building	Romantic Hideaway	
VERMONT									
Arlington Inn	✓	✓		✓		✓	✓	✓	
The Battenkill Inn	✓	✓		✓			✓		
Beaver Pond Farm Inn		✓		✓		✓	✓		
Black Lantern Inn	✓	✓		✓		✓	✓	✓	
Blueberry Hill Inn	✓	✓				✓		✓	
The Chester Inn at Long Last		✓				✓	✓		
Cornucopia		✓						✓	
The Deerhill Inn		✓				✓		✓	
Eaglebrook of Grafton		✓		✓			✓	✓	
Edson Hill Manor		✓						✓	
1811 House		✓					✓	✓	
Four Columns	✓	✓					✓	✓	
Fox Hall Inn		✓	✓	✓			✓	✓	
The Gables Inn	✓	✓		✓		✓		✓	
Governor's Inn		✓				✓	✓	✓	
Green Trails Inn		✓	✓	✓		✓	✓		
Hickory Ridge House		✓		✓			✓	✓	
Hill Farm Inn		✓		✓				✓	
Inn at Montpelier		✓				✓	✓		
The Inn at Sawmill Farm		✓				✓		✓	
The Inn at the Round Barn Farm		✓					✓	✓	
The Inn at Ormsby Hill	✓	✓					✓	✓	
Inn at Weathersfield		✓				✓	✓	✓	
Inn on the Common		✓				✓		✓	
Juniper Hill Inn		✓				✓	✓	✓	

Luxurious	Pets Allowed	No Smoking Indoors	Good Place for Families	Near Arts Festivals	Beach Nearby	Cross-Country Ski Trail	Golf within 5 Miles	Fitness Facilities	Good Biking Terrain	Skiing	Horseback Riding	Tennis	Swimming on Premises	Hiking Nearby
		✓		✓	✓		✓		✓	✓	✓	✓		✓
		✓		✓			✓		✓	✓				✓
		✓	✓	✓		✓	✓		✓	✓				✓
		✓							✓	✓		✓		✓
		✓				✓	✓		✓	✓			✓	✓
		✓	✓	✓			✓		✓			✓		
✓		✓		✓			✓		✓	✓				✓
✓		✓		✓			✓		✓	✓		✓	✓	✓
✓		✓		✓		✓			✓	✓				
		✓	✓	✓			✓			✓	✓		✓	✓
✓		✓		✓			✓		✓	✓				✓
✓		✓		✓		✓			✓				✓	✓
		✓		✓			✓		✓	✓			✓	✓
		✓	✓	✓		✓	✓		✓	✓			✓	✓
✓		✓		✓					✓	✓				✓
		✓	✓	✓		✓	✓		✓	✓				✓
		✓		✓		✓			✓					
	✓	✓	✓	✓		✓	✓		✓	✓				✓
✓		✓		✓					✓					
✓		✓		✓		✓	✓		✓	✓		✓	✓	
✓		✓		✓		✓	✓		✓	✓			✓	
✓		✓		✓			✓		✓	✓				✓
		✓				✓		✓	✓					
✓		✓	✓			✓	✓		✓	✓		✓	✓	✓
✓		✓				✓			✓	✓				✓

Special Features at a Glance

Name of Property	Accessible for People with Disabilities	Antiques	On the Water	Good Value	Car Not Necessary	Full Meal Service	Historic Building	Romantic Hideaway	
Kedron Valley Inn		✓		✓		✓	✓	✓	
Lareau Farm Country Inn		✓		✓			✓		
Molly Stark Inn		✓		✓				✓	
The Old Tavern at Grafton	✓	✓		✓		✓	✓	✓	
Parker House		✓				✓	✓	✓	
Rabbit Hill Inn	✓	✓	✓			✓	✓	✓	
Reluctant Panther	✓	✓				✓		✓	
South Shire Inn	✓	✓		✓			✓	✓	
Swift House Inn	✓	✓				✓	✓	✓	
West Mountain Inn	✓	✓		✓		✓	✓	✓	
Whetstone Inn		✓		✓			✓	✓	
Wilburton Inn		✓				✓	✓	✓	
Wildflower Inn	✓	✓		✓					
The Willard Street Inn		✓		✓	✓		✓	✓	
Windham Hill Inn		✓				✓	✓	✓	
Ye Olde England Inn		✓				✓			

Luxurious	Pets Allowed	No Smoking Indoors	Good Place for Families	Beach Nearby	Cross-Country Ski Trails	Golf Within 5 Miles	Fitness Facilities	Near Wineries	Good Biking Terrain	Skiing	Tennis	Swimming on Premises	Conference Facilities	Hiking Nearby
	✓	✓	✓	✓	✓	✓	✓		✓	✓	✓	✓	✓	
		✓	✓	✓		✓	✓		✓	✓	✓		✓	✓
		✓	✓	✓		✓	✓		✓	✓				✓
	✓	✓		✓		✓			✓	✓		✓	✓	✓
✓		✓		✓			✓		✓					
✓		✓				✓			✓	✓				✓
✓		✓		✓		✓	✓		✓	✓				✓
✓		✓							✓					
✓		✓	✓	✓		✓			✓					✓
✓		✓	✓	✓		✓			✓	✓				✓
	✓	✓		✓		✓			✓	✓				
✓		✓	✓	✓		✓	✓		✓	✓		✓	✓	✓
		✓	✓			✓			✓	✓	✓	✓	✓	✓
✓		✓		✓			✓		✓					
✓		✓		✓		✓			✓	✓				✓
	✓	✓	✓	✓		✓	✓		✓	✓		✓	✓	

Connecticut

Connecticut

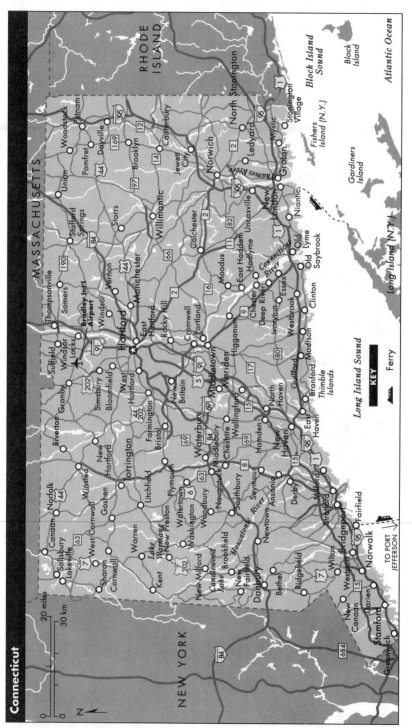

The Southwestern Coast

The Maples Inn

Much of Connecticut's shoreline between Greenwich and New Haven is an artery of the urban sprawl that radiates from New York City. Beyond the bustle of commerce, however, there are densely wooded communities of stately historic homes and winding, elm-shaded roads. Fairfield County, despite its "commuter country" image, has a pace of its own, and the odds against encountering the so-called New York attitude in southwestern Connecticut are definitely in your favor.

Long before the environmental movement took hold, people in Fairfield County established wilderness preserves and nature centers, principally in the upland sections rather than directly on the coast. Today, on hundreds of safeguarded acres, these refuges from the overbuilt downtown areas offer you well-marked trails for hiking, bird-watching, horseback riding, and bicycling as well as educational exhibits and hands-on activities for children.

In recent years the most congested of the region's metropolitan areas, after suffering serious decline, have changed direction, improving in appearance and civic fortune. Stamford has gone the big-city route, with tall hotel and corporate towers turning its downtown into a slick steel, glass, and cement jungle. South Norwalk, fondly known now as SoNo, has taken on new life around its acclaimed Maritime Aquarium, with trendy art galleries, boutiques, and restaurants cheek by jowl with expensive condominiums in renovated warehouses.

Places to Go, Sights to See

Maritime Aquarium at Norwalk (10 N. Water St., Norwalk, tel. 203/852–0700). One of the state's most popular attractions, this state-of-the-art, 5-acre, aquarium/museum/IMAX theater complex on the west bank of the Norwalk River highlights the maritime history and marine life of Long Island Sound through exhibits, educational programs, and big-screen entertainment.

Stamford Museum and Nature Center (39 Scofieldtown Rd., Stamford, tel. 203/322–1646). This 118-acre preserve with its popular nature trails also features changing exhibits on natural history, art, and Americana as well as a permanent exhibit on Native American life. It's all centered around a 19th-century working farm.

Weir Farm (735 Nod Hill Rd., Wilton, tel. 203/834–1896). Connecticut's first and only national park is dedicated to the life and art of American painter J. Alden Weir. The park's 60 wooded acres comprise studios, Weir's Federal house, exhibits, period gardens, and guided tours of Weir's painting sites and studio.

Yale University. As befits a prestigious seat of learning, the Yale campus is chockablock with history. The university offers free guided walking tours (tel. 203/432–2300), during which you can glimpse the places where Nathan Hale, William Howard Taft, and President and Mrs. Clinton once studied.

Beaches

The numerous sandy strips along the shore may be marked PRIVATE and FOR RESIDENTS ONLY, but this restriction generally applies to parking only, for which there is a fee. If you can walk or bicycle to a beach, usually no one minds you settling down for some quiet sunbathing. The big public beach in the region is **Sherwood Island State Park** (Exit 18 off I–95, Westport, tel. 203/226–6983), which features a 1½-mi sweep of sandy beach, food concessions, two large picnic groves close to the water, and parking.

Shopping

Main Street in Westport is a trendy shopper's paradise. Stores include The Gap, J. Crew, Coach, Laura Ashley, Eddie Bauer, and Brooks Brothers—all the names you know and love.

Restaurants

Greenwich, New Haven, Stamford, and Westport have all emerged in recent years as champions of innovative cuisine. In Greenwich **Restaurant Jean-Louis** (61 Lewis St., tel. 203/622–8450) is among the nation's top French restaurants. In New Haven the legendary pizza at **Frank Pepe's** (157 Wooster St., tel. 203/865–5762) is worth the wait—as much as two hours some nights—but **Pika Tapas Cafe** (39 High St., tel. 203/865–1933) is the better choice for a special occasion. Its vast (and delicious) assortment of Spanish tapas will dazzle you. Summer Street in downtown Stamford has become a restaurant row with terrific purveyors of Austrian food at **Amadeus** (201 Summer St., tel. 203/348–7775), Indian food at **Meera** (227 Summer St., tel. 203/975–0477), and upscale Mexican food at **La Hacienda** (222 Summer St., tel. 203/324–0577). The fried whole-belly clams are legendary at Westport's **Mansion Clam House** (541 Riverside Ave., tel. 203/454–7979), or for the sophisticated tastes of the Mediterranean, don't miss the deftly seasoned fare at **Cafe Christina** (1 Main St., tel. 203/221–7950).

Nightlife and the Arts

Bridgeport's **Downtown Cabaret Theatre** (tel. 203/576–1636) has a steady audience for its informal, lively, dinner-theater productions. The **Stamford Center for the Arts** (tel. 203/325–4466) offers everything from comedy shows and top-notch musicals to film fests and a young-audience series. New Haven's **Long Wharf Theatre** (tel. 203/787–4282) and **Yale Repertory Theatre** (tel. 203/432–1234) stage a range of classic and new comedies and tragedies. Legendary **Toad's Place** (tel. 203/624–8263) has been drawing crowds for years to hear both classic and alternative rock bands. Spectacle as well as sport is found at **Milford Jai Alai** (tel. 203/877–4242), where you can simply watch or wager on this spirited game.

Reservations Services

Bed & Breakfast, Ltd. (Box 216, New Haven 06513, tel. 203/469–3260), **Covered Bridge Bed & Breakfast Reservation Service** (Box 447, Norfolk 06058, tel. 860/542–5944), **Nutmeg Bed & Breakfast Agency** (Box 1117, West Hartford 06127, tel. 860/236–6698 or 800/727–7592).

Visitor Information

Coastal Fairfield County Convention and Visitors Bureau (297 West Ave., The Gate Lodge–Mathews Park, Norwalk 06850, tel. 203/854–7825 or 800/866–7925), **Greater New Haven Convention and Visitors District** (1 Long Wharf Dr., Suite 7, New Haven 06511, tel. 203/777–8550 or 800/332–7829).

The Cotswold Inn

76 Myrtle Ave., Westport 06880, tel. 203/226-3766, fax 203/221-0098

For years honeymooners have been known to nest at the Cotswold Inn, a charming gray-cedar-shake cottage with a proliferation of gables and skylights. Nowadays you're also likely to encounter Europeans touring the Connecticut shoreline and New Yorkers looking for a short break from urbanity (Manhattan is just 50 mi away).

Though the steep gables, stone porches, and neatly manicured hedges and flower gardens recall England's Cotswold region, rooms capture the essence of 18th-century Connecticut, with reproduction Chippendale and Queen Anne furnishings—highboys, mule chests, wing chairs. Two rooms have canopy beds, the suite has a fireplace, and all are spruced up daily with fresh flowers. A common living room is made welcoming with about a dozen dried-flower arrangements and soft classical music. Here a Continental breakfast of fresh muffins, fruit, yogurt, and gourmet coffees is laid out; wine, cordials, and snacks are set out here every evening. More museumlike than it is homey (and not a place to bring young children), the Cotswold is perfect if you're looking for the efficiency and privacy of a small hotel *and* the intimacy of a B&B.

🏠 *3 doubles with bath, 1 suite. Air-conditioning, cable TV, phones, terry-cloth robes, hair dryers in rooms. $175–$245; Continental breakfast. AE, MC, V. No pets.*

Harbor House Inn

165 Shore Rd., Old Greenwich 06870, tel. 203/637-0145, fax 203/698-0943

Around the turn of the century, there was an enormous beach resort hotel called the Old Greenwich Inn. To house the servants of all the people who stayed there, a subdued Victorian beachfront cottage with three stories and many gables was built nearby. The Old Greenwich disappeared, but the cottage endured—transformed into a comfortable guest house by the Stuttig family and managed today by Dawn Brown under the watchful eye of her mother, Dolly Stuttig. There are several spacious rooms around the massive lobby, and bits of stained glass filter the light here and on the second and third floors. Having grown up in the business, Dawn runs a tight ship. Unfortunately, in the interest of efficiency, the decor is rather bland. Walls are covered with modern veneer paneling, and the furniture, though comfortable, is department-store standard. Simplicity is the rule, extending to the fully equipped bathrooms. The exception is the lobby, with its grand piano, stately antiques, and lush Asian carpets. Harbor House Inn specializes in long-term stays by corporate executives.

🏠 *17 doubles with bath, 6 doubles share 2 baths. Air-conditioning, cable TV/VCRs, minirefrigerators, coffeemakers, phones in rooms; laundry facilities; bicycles; video library. $99–$140; Continental breakfast. AE, DC, MC, V. No smoking, no pets.*

The Homestead Inn

420 Field Point Rd., Greenwich 06830, tel. and fax 203/869-7500

Just south of I-95, the Connecticut Turnpike, on a tree-shaded street in Greenwich, sits a wooden frame house with an enclosed Victorian wraparound porch, an Italianate cupola, and ornate gingerbread trim. All the common rooms on the ground level get a lot of use from overnight guests and regular patrons of the celebrated restaurant, where new owner-chef Thomas Henkelmann's up-to-the-minute, fine, French cuisine is already garnering rave reviews. Yet the public areas, which contain a mix of fine antiques and country charm, sophistication, and nostalgia, still have a pristine sheen that comes only from superior maintenance.

In the main house there are 13 guest rooms, each with its own mix of Victorian and Queen Anne antiques and reproductions. The Bride's Room has a pale blue pencil-post bed complemented by gaily printed flower-basket wallpaper and orange wing chairs. Rooms in the 19th-century outbuilding are decorated in much the same manner as those in the main house. The Birdcage Room is typical; it has an antique blue-and-white French birdcage whose colors are echoed by a painted chest of drawers and an upholstered boudoir chair.

At press time (spring 1998), Thomas and his wife, Theresa Carroll, had just taken over the inn but had already whitewashed the facade and painted the shutters a rich green. They were planning renovations of the common and guest rooms—work was slated to take place gradually so they would still be able accommodate guests.

🏨 *14 doubles, 3 singles with bath; 6 suites. Air-conditioning, cable TV, phones, terry-cloth robes in rooms; meeting rooms. $150–$350. AE, DC, MC, V. No pets.*

The Inn at National Hall

2 Post Rd. W, Westport 06880, tel. 203/ 221–1351 or 800/628–4255, fax 203/221– 0276

The self-important name belies the whimsical, exotic interior of this towering redbrick Italianate on the downtown banks of the Saugatuck River. Built by Lee Tauck, the owner of the renowned tour company, Tauck Tours, the Inn opened in 1993, becoming the second truly world-class luxury hotel in Connecticut—after the equally sumptuous Mayflower Inn, in Washington, Connecticut, which opened in 1992.

Each of the rooms here is a study in innovative restoration, wall stenciling, and decorative design. The trompe l'oeil touches are evident from the moment you enter the lobby elevator, whose walls are painted to look like tome-filled bookshelves. A tour of the lounge and lobby reveals an exquisite furniture collection. Note the 300-year-old Swedish grandfather clock by the reception desk and also the chandelier, which once hung in London's Savoy Hotel, over the table in the small, elegant, conference room. Downstairs is a classic snooker table, imported from England. The hallways feature fine hand stenciling and delicate wood paneling.

Rooms and suites are magnificent—four of them have sleeping lofts, and several have 12-ft-high windows. All have opulent four-poster beds adorned with corollas or canopies and have limestone bathrooms with sleek marble baths, heated towel bars, hair dryers, plush Turkish-cotton bathrobes, and slippers. All rooms are also completely soundproof and have modem and fax lines.

The Turkistan Suite is probably the largest, with a two-story floor-to-ceiling bookcase, 12-ft-high windows overlooking the river below, and, behind the loft's bowfront balcony, an ornate king-size four-poster with an Egyptian-print canopy and painted valance. The Equestrian Suite (its walls are covered with horse stenciling) has an armoire fitted with a custom-made kitchenette, its own Jacuzzi, an enormous bathroom, and a remote-controlled gas fireplace. A smaller suite, The Saugatuck, offers expansive river views as well as French doors that separate the bedroom from the living area—perfect for entertaining. The Acorn Room is one of the smallest, but it's still larger than what you'd find in a typical first-rate hotel.

With its Corinthian columns and tasseled curtain swags, the Restaurant at National Hall, on the lushly decorated ground floor, sets the stage for fine— sometimes exotic—Continental fare. The champagne jazz brunch on Sunday is an additional pleasure.

🏨 *8 doubles with bath, 7 suites. Restaurant; air-conditioning, cable TV/VCRs, phones, refrigerators in* rooms; kitchenette, fireplace in 1 suite; 24-hr room service; meeting facilities. $195–$395, suites $395–$525; Continental breakfast. AE, DC, MC, V. No smoking, no pets.

The Maples Inn

179 Oenoke Ridge, New Canaan 06840, tel. 203/966–2927, fax 203/966–5003

From its location on Oenoke Ridge, just a short drive from New Canaan's downtown, the vast, white-trimmed, yellow-clapboard Maples Inn reveals only a few of its 13 gables. Its many windows (too many to count) blink invitingly at night and have been welcoming guests since Cynthia T. Haas took over as owner in early 1982.

Cynthia, a longtime New Canaan resident, had always wanted to run an inn. When her chance came, she made sweeping changes, rearranging rooms, bathrooms, closets, even walls. Her efforts have created a subdued but elegant, warm, and romantic atmosphere.

All the guest rooms have canopied, four-poster, queen-size beds and numerous antiques from Cynthia's own collection. The presence of such modern equipment as phones and TVs is never intrusive. Mahogany chests, gilt frames, and brass lamps all gleam, and the imaginative use of light floral fabrics and paper fans is an education in design. The fully equipped four-bedroom cottage displays the same sensitivity to beauty and comfort.

You can help yourself to breakfast in the Mural Room, with its three chandeliers and walls painted with striking images of New Canaan during each season. French doors open onto a wicker-filled wraparound porch—an ideal dining spot in warm weather—that overlooks a deep lawn with venerable maples.

The small apartments and the cottage seem to encourage long-term stays by families, and youngsters, generally respectful of the premises, are made to feel at home in the friendly, informal atmosphere. You might well be offered a treat from a box of goodies in the front desk drawer. The Maples Inn is that kind of place.

⌂ 7 doubles with bath, 4 suites (1 with screened-in porch), 10 apartments. Air-conditioning, cable TV, phones in rooms; minirefrigerators in most rooms; working fireplace in 2 apartments. $135–$250; Continental breakfast. AE, MC, V. No pets.

Roger Sherman Inn

195 Oenoke Ridge, New Canaan 06840, tel. 203/966–4541, fax 203/966–0503

The Roger Sherman's winding porch faces a broad tree-lined avenue and invites relaxation. The white, shingle-and-clapboard, center-chimney Colonial dates from 1740 and has functioned as an inn since 1925. Its present owners, Thomas and Kay Weilenmann, took over just last year and have already refurbished extensively. The inn's popular restaurant serves contemporary Continental cuisine and Swiss specialties (Thomas's last position was as general manager at the Nova-Park Hotel in Zurich) and is widely used for social events and business meetings. Dark paneling, hunting prints, and a blazing hearth in the bar make it a favorite indoor gathering place.

Guest rooms are furnished with Colonial reproductions; fine botanical prints; and such modern amenities as wall-to-wall carpeting, TVs, and shiny plastic ice buckets. Antique touches include the woodwork, the bric-a-brac, and the uneven floors. A head-to-toe refurbishment of the inn's carriage house is planned for spring 1998, and this will add nine rooms.

⌂ 7 doubles with bath, 1 2-bedroom suite. Restaurant and lounge with live piano music; air-conditioning, cable TV, minibars, phones in rooms; dry cleaning. $135, suite $300; Continental breakfast. AE, DC, MC, V. No smoking in rooms, no pets.

Silvermine Tavern

194 Perry Ave., Norwalk 06850, tel. 203/847-4558, fax 203/847-9171

Silvermine is a pre-Revolutionary town that lies within the borders of Norwalk, New Canaan, and Wilton. The Tavern (part of which dates from 1642), the Country Store, the Coach House, and the Old Mill are all clustered at the intersection of Silvermine and Perry avenues in Norwalk, just north of the Merritt Parkway.

If he has a moment to spare in his busy schedule, innkeeper Frank Whitman, Jr., can fill you in on local history. His family has been running things here since 1955, and he grew up within the solid post-and-beam walls of the Colonial building at the heart of the present-day Tavern. Frank's eyes never seem to rest because he never lets up on the high standards he sets for the food and accommodations.

Though best known for its romantic restaurant, which overlooks the Silvermine River and the millpond, the inn also has wonderful guest rooms in the main building and across the road above the Country Store. (Note to collectors: they carry Mary Hadley Pottery here.) The Tavern's common areas and multiple dining rooms have unusual displays of primitive paintings, store signs, prints, and Early American tools and utensils. The guest rooms, with their own complement of antique furnishings, have an equally pleasant atmosphere. The configuration of these rooms has evolved over the ages, and the odd shapes only add to the charm. Room T-8 is entered through the bathroom but is particularly cozy once you're inside. Three rooms have tubs but no showers because of the slanted ceilings. Wide-plank floors have hooked rugs to bridge the cracks of age, and starched white curtains grace the small, multipaned windows.

Be sure to eat at least one meal here (and try the Tavern's signature honey buns).

Traditional New England favorites are given some new slants: The duckling is semiboneless and served with rhubarb and dried cherry chutney, and the preparation of the filet mignon and salmon change seasonally. Sunday brunch on the tree-shaded outdoor deck is a local tradition. The Whitmans have mapped out a 2-mi walking tour of Silvermine that's ideal for an after-dinner stroll.

▦ *10 doubles with bath. Restaurant; air-conditioning in 6 rooms. $90–$110; Continental breakfast. AE, DC, MC, V. No pets. Closed Tues. year-round.*

The Stanton House Inn

76 Maple Ave., Greenwich 06830, tel. 203/869-2110, fax 203/629-2116

Off busy Route 1, near the imposing Second Congregational Church, a hairpin right turn up Maple Avenue leads you to a white Federal-style house built in 1840 and enlarged in 1899 by architect Stanford White. Doreen Pearson, a former registered nurse, and her husband, Tog, a banking executive, have transformed this once somewhat seedy boardinghouse into a comfortable B&B.

A number of top-floor rooms share bathroom facilities, but the spacious bedrooms on the sprawling second floor each have their own. Room 28, with its Wedgwood color scheme, has a working fireplace and a private deck. All the rooms were decorated by Doreen, who claims expertise in dealing with upholsterers, carpenters, furniture restorers, and all manner of artisans. The results are reflected in a variety of tasteful, bright, print bedspreads and window draperies. Doreen's touch is also apparent in the formal first-floor drawing room and dining room, where coffee and tea service is available all day and where sherry is set out in the afternoon. A Continental breakfast is served on the brick patio by the pool once the weather brightens. Parents might have a hard time keeping young children amused here, though preteens and teens should be fine.

⊞ *23 doubles with bath, 2 doubles share bath, 1 suite. Air-conditioning, cable TV, phones, hair dryers in rooms; wet bar in 7 rooms; small conference room; outdoor pool. $85–$139, suite $175; Continental breakfast. AE, D, MC, V. No smoking, no pets. 2-night minimum weekends.*

Three Chimneys Inn

1201 Chapel St., New Haven 06511, tel. 203/789–1201, fax 203/776–7363

Running along the New Haven Green and into the heart of the Yale University campus, Chapel Street seems an infinite stretch of shops, old hotels, bookstores, and restaurants until you come to a surprise: Behind a neatly kept garden stands a freshly painted green, white, and pink Victorian mansion, complete with gingerbread trim and a carpeted stairway flanked by potted geraniums. It's amazing that this 1870 structure never fell to the wrecker's ball as its neighbors undoubtedly did; it's equally mind-boggling that someone had the vision to restore it and convert it into a thriving, much-needed lodging in this vibrant college town.

When the owners took over this establishment, formerly the Inn at Chapel West, they were determined to create a small hotel of uncommon luxury that would be ideal both for couples seeking a romantic retreat and for businesspeople. They have succeeded. Each room has been completely renovated and has posh Georgian and Federal furnishings, grand mahogany four-poster beds, oversize armoires, Chippendale-style desks, and Asian rugs whose colors are reflected in the rich, warm tones of the decor. A basket of homemade cookies (chocolate chip, if you're lucky) and tea is the perfect welcoming touch.

The inn also offers complete conference facilities for groups of up to 75 (depending on the function), with catered meals—so a whiff of something appetizing wafting through its doors at mealtimes is to be expected. You can lounge in both the breakfast room and the library; each has double fireplaces. Sherry is best enjoyed in the library and the inn's French toast made with Grand Marnier and orange juice in the breakfast room.

The staff here is delighted to recommend restaurants in New Haven or make arrangements for theater tickets, a university tour, or secretarial or baby-sitting services. Such personal attention makes the inn an urban oasis.

⊞ *10 doubles with bath. Air-conditioning, cable TV, phones in rooms; free parking. $155; full breakfast. AE, D, MC, V. No smoking, no pets. 2-night minimum weekends and holidays.*

Litchfield County South and Ridgefield

Hopkins Inn

Southern Litchfield County contains a mixture of small towns and urban centers typical of the state, but its many lakes and rivers are what truly set it apart. When the snow thaws, the anglers start counting the days until they can legally plunge into rivers such as the Housatonic, Aspetuck, and Bantam. The shores of Waramaug and Candlewood lakes are equally seductive, luring sunbathers, boating enthusiasts, and lovers of various types of water sports.

Many visitors come in search of treasures at the numerous antiques shops along the highways and byways. Woodbury, Kent, and New Preston all have well-traveled antiques trails. Litchfield, the county seat, is another top choice—one with both antiques and a little of the area's history. Both it and Ridgefield, in northern Fairfield County, are classic Yankee towns where prosperous merchants and landowners built monumental residences. Many of these mansions have been taken over by preservation and historical societies and are open to the public. Charity tours—announced on signposts, bulletin boards, and in the local press—open the doors to many other currently occupied dwellings.

The climate in this part of the Nutmeg State favors the growing of grapes, and consequently a wine-making industry has developed. Several vineyards welcome visitors to sample and perhaps purchase the product of their labors.

Places to Go, Sights to See

Aldrich Museum of Contemporary Art (258 Main St., Ridgefield, tel. 203/438–4519). This world-class gallery has one of the best sculpture gardens in the Northeast as well as changing exhibits, lectures, concerts, and films.

Lourdes of Litchfield Shrine (Rte. 118, Litchfield, tel. 860/567–1041). The grotto of Lourdes, France, is reproduced on this 35-acre shrine maintained by the Montfort Missionaries. During pilgrimage season, from May through mid-October, outdoor mass is held Sunday at 11:30; Holy Hour is at 3. The grounds are open year-round, and picnickers are welcome any time.

The Silo (44 Upland Rd., off Rte. 202, New Milford, tel. 860/355–0300). Band leader Skitch Henderson and his wife, Ruth, own and operate this wonderful silo and barn packed with "objets d'cookery," gourmet goodies and sauces, and arts and crafts.

White Flower Farm (Rte. 63, south of Litchfield Green, tel. 860/567–8789). When word gets around that the azaleas are in bloom at this world-class horticultural mecca, there's bound to be a slowdown on Route 63 south of Litchfield. Its 10 acres of gardens and 30 acres of growing fields peak from midsummer to September, but green-thumb pros and amateurs alike flock here from early spring to late December, drawn partially by the lure of its widely circulated catalog. It doesn't disappoint.

White Memorial Foundation (Rte. 202, 2 mi west of Litchfield Green, tel. 860/567–0857). The state's largest nature center and wildlife sanctuary offers visitors 4,000 acres containing 35 mi of trails for hiking, horseback riding, and cross-country skiing. There are also a conservation center with natural-history exhibits, a library, and a gift shop. Open year-round, it's a great place to marvel at the fall foliage.

Beaches

Virtually every town that sits on a lake has a public beach where all are welcome. The hitch is you need a local parking permit. Luckily, you can walk or bicycle from most of the lodgings listed here to their own beach or to one nearby.

Several of the area's lakes are home to scenic state parks, including Candlewood Lake's **Squantz Pond State Park** (New Fairfield, tel. 203/797–4165) and **Lake Waramaug State Park** (New Preston/Kent, tel. 860/868–0220 or 860/868–2592).

Restaurants

Hands down, the best-known restaurant in the region is James O'Shea's **West Street Grill** (43 West St., tel. 860/567–3885), in Litchfield. This small, unpretentious dining room is the favorite of local glitterati for its imaginative take on regional American cuisine. **G. W. Tavern** (20 Bee Brook Rd., tel. 860/868–6633), in Washington, is devotedly Colonial in both cuisine—roast beef with Yorkshire pudding is a star example—and atmosphere. If you're looking for a bite in New Preston near Lake Waramaug's many inns, try **Oliva** (18 E. Shore Rd., tel. 860/868–1787), whose bright little patio overlooks antiques shops. Two other great eateries in the region are Woodbury's **Good News Café** (649 Main St. S, tel. 203/266–4663), whose kitchen is presided over by renowned chef Carole Peck, and New Milford's **Bistro Café** (31 Bank St., tel. 860/355–3266); though both serve outstanding new American cuisine, the Good News Café serves more inventive dishes.

Nightlife and the Arts

New Milford's **Poor Henry's** (tel. 860/355–2274) is the most popular of several bars around Bank Street and the railroad station. **Gateway's Candlewood Playhouse** (tel. 203/746–4441), close by the shores of Candlewood Lake in New Fairfield, is where summer stock once flourished and where current theatrical hits are eagerly applauded today.

Reservations Services

Bed & Breakfast, Ltd. (Box 216, New Haven 06513, tel. 203/469–3260), **Covered Bridge Bed & Breakfast Reservation Service** (Box 447, Norfolk 06058, tel. 860/542–5944), **Nutmeg Bed & Breakfast Agency** (Box 1117, West Hartford 06127, tel. 860/236–6698 or 800/727–7592).

Visitor Information

Housatonic Valley Tourism District (46 Main St., Box 406, Danbury 06810, tel. 203/743–0546 or 800/841–4488), **Litchfield Hills Travel Council** (Box 968, Litchfield 06759, tel. 860/567–4506).

The Boulders

*E. Shore Rd. (Rte. 45), New Preston
06777, tel. 860/868–0541 or 800/552–6853,
fax 860/868–1925*

Built in 1895 as a private house, the
stone and shingle Boulders inn, with its
carriage house and four guest houses,
sits on a gentle slope with panoramic
views of Lake Waramaug. The innkeepers, Kees and Ulla Adema, came from
Holland and Germany, respectively, in
the '60s, and now that their children are
grown and away at school, they're able
to devote themselves exclusively to the
running of the inn. A bit of European
charm seems appropriate to this hillside
retreat.

The guest rooms are a curious—though
luxurious—mixture, with picture windows, Asian rugs, antique Victorian
furniture and bric-a-brac, as well as reproduction and overstuffed pieces. The
eight rooms in the guest houses up the
hill have private decks and working
fireplaces. The carriage house has three
well-furnished rooms with private entrances and fireplaces.

In the main inn building, the sumptuous
living room and adjoining TV library
both overlook the lake and welcome you
for relaxed reading, conversation with
other guests, and spectacular sunsets.
A recreation room in the basement has
a pool table, an antique pinball machine,
darts, and an assortment of games.
Across the road the inn has a private
stretch of waterfront suitable for swimming and a beach house with a hanging
wicker swing for passing peaceful moments. The more adventurous may set
forth in a canoe or a paddleboat, both
provided free.

At dinner in the glass-enclosed Lake
Room, you can choose from among several outstanding dishes, which may include roasted free-range chicken with
tarragon, lemon essence, carrot chips, and
vegetable fricassee or pan-seared Chilean
sea bass with Swiss chard, leeks, diced
potato, saffron, and aioli with red-wine
fumet. The menu changes often, so be
prepared for some imaginative specials.

Running the inn is a full-time job, but
Kees and Ulla squeeze in time for their
hobbies. He is an avid stamp collector
who exhibits internationally, and Ulla's
specialty can be seen in the meticulously
cut lamp shades used throughout the inn.

▦ *15 doubles with bath, 2 suites. Restaurant; air-conditioning, hair dryers
in rooms; double Jacuzzis in 4 guest-
house rooms; minirefrigerators, coffeemakers in carriage house and guest
houses; lake swimming; boating; tennis
court; bicycles and helmets; hiking trail.
$250–$300; full breakfast. AE, MC, V.
No smoking, no pets. Children under
age 12 by special arrangement. 2-night
minimum weekends.*

The Curtis House

*506 Main St. (Rte. 6), Woodbury 06798,
tel. 203/263–2101*

Connecticut's oldest inn (1754), located
at the start of Woodbury's antiques row,
may also be its cheapest: Some rooms,
even with private bath, are less than $50.
The three-story, white-clapboard Colonial inn, run by the Hardisty family, has
seen dozens of alterations and renovations—including a complete $400 over-
haul in 1900—but the TVs in some rooms
look to be from the Ed Sullivan era; the
phones are rotary-dial; and the floorboards, which still creak like whoopee
cushions, are charmingly uneven.
(There's not a spot in the inn where a
marble placed on the floor won't zip
across the room.) Your quarters are
likely to have a canopy bed; floral wallpaper; a stuffed chair; what you'd swear
is the braided rug you last saw in your
grandmother's living room; and, if you
reserve a room with a private bath, a
claw-foot tub. A fireplace roars downstairs, and a wonderfully cozy restaurant serves heavy but filling New
England fare, such as Yankee pot roast,
turkey potpie, and a rich rice-stuffed

duckling in cherry-bourbon sauce. An additional four rooms have recently been added in the former carriage house, connected to the main grounds by a footbridge.

🏨 *12 doubles with bath, 6 doubles share bath. Restaurant; air-conditioning, cable TV in some rooms. $40–$123; Continental breakfast extra. D, MC, V. No pets. 2-night minimum weekends.*

The Elms Inn

500 Main St., Ridgefield 06877, tel. and fax 203/438-2541

The impressive Colonial frame house that is the Elms Inn on Main Street was once the home of a cabinetmaker, who built it in 1760 near the site of the Battle of Ridgefield. After the war, in 1799, it became an inn, which now includes an adjacent building erected in 1850. Since 1951 it has been operated by the Scala family, who in 1983 did a total renovation and have continued upgrading ever since.

By carefully combining antiques, reproductions, and modern fixtures, the Scalas have created an atmospheric and comfortable stop for weary, hungry travelers. They have recently joined forces with New York City restaurateur Brendan Walsh (of Arizona 206) to rework the restaurant. The new Elms Restaurant and Tavern, each with a distinctive Colonial atmosphere, feature seasonally changing menus of new American cuisine. You might choose the likes of skillet-roasted organic chicken with fresh morel bread stuffing or maple-thyme grilled loin of venison.

Although the decorating approach to the guest rooms varies from "olde days" to modern hotel, each room is furnished with such appropriate Colonial-style touches as pineapple-stenciled wallpaper, plank flooring, and hobnail spreads on lace-canopied four-poster beds. Most rooms have queen-size beds and good reading lights, and comfortable Hitchcock armchairs are found throughout.

Room 12 has a daydream-inducing window seat that overlooks the inn's expansive lawn.

The idea of lodging smack in the middle of town may not at first seem appealing, but the Elms is on a broad avenue lined by tree-shaded mansions and close to pleasures such as band concerts in the park, antiques shops, boutiques, and historic sites. In fact, the antique map in the main dining room and the Revolutionary War relics scattered about the premises might even stir up your most patriotic sentiments.

🏨 *20 doubles with bath, 4 suites. Restaurant; room service; air-conditioning, cable TV, phones in rooms. $110–$160; Continental breakfast. AE, DC, MC, V. No smoking, no pets.*

The Homestead Inn

5 Elm St., New Milford 06776, tel. 860/354-4080, fax 860/354-7046

This rambling, white-clapboard Victorian inn near the north end of the Village Green is hard to miss. Innkeepers Rolf and Peggy Hammer, formerly a marketing executive and a physical therapist, took over the inn, which has been in operation continuously since 1928, in 1985 after they retired. They now devote themselves to their guests in the main house—which dates from 1853 and which, legend has it, hosted Arthur Miller and Marilyn Monroe in the '50s—and the adjacent six-room motel they call the Treadwell House. The bedrooms are decorated with floral-print curtains and bedspreads, and the four-poster, pencil-post, and Jenny Lind beds seem quite at home with an assortment of antiques and country-style bric-a-brac. A hearty Continental breakfast is served in the dark-beamed living room with its antique Steinway piano and works by local artists. It's especially cheerful in the winter, with a blazing fire in the hearth. In summer you may prefer to eat breakfast on the wicker-furnished front porch that overlooks the green.

🏨 *14 doubles with bath. Air-condition-ing, cable TV, phones in rooms. $78–$101; Continental breakfast buffet. AE, D, DC, MC, V. No pets. 2-night minimum week-ends, May–Oct., and holidays.*

Hopkins Inn

22 Hopkins Rd., New Preston 06777, tel. 860/868–7295, fax 860/868–7464

This grand, yellow and white, 1847 Vic-torian on a hill overlooking Lake Wara-maug has grown from a 19th-century summer boardinghouse to a delightful 20th-century country inn. As you drive up the short street that leads to both the inn and the Hopkins Winery (this is pos-sibly the only inn in Connecticut with vineyards and a winery at its doorstep) note the flag flying over the front entry; the countless mullioned windows flanked by shutters; and all the gables, awnings, roofs, and porches. But presiding serenely over everything, the present-day innkeepers Franz and Beth Schober are the picture of efficiency.

At the inn, where dining has become cel-ebrated, Franz is usually found in the kitchen, whence come the Austrian and Swiss dishes that form the centerpiece of the menu. His insistence on fresh in-gredients extends to the maintenance of a fish tank stocked with trout, and he is also responsible for the extensive selec-tion of wine that is carefully stored in the inn's cellar.

Beth's touch is seen just about every-where else. She was a university librar-ian before taking over the inn in 1977, and her organizational skills show up in its smooth operation.

Each guest room has a unique shape and decor, though Colonial-print wallpapers and fabrics and light florals are used ex-tensively throughout. Furniture runs the gamut of country styles, with em-phasis on crisp, ruffled bed linens; sturdy, comfortable brass beds; good chairs for reading; and a variety of an-tique decorative pieces scattered about.

A two-bedroom apartment has been re-cently been added in the annex.

You can relax by the fireplace in the cozy, Victorian-style living room on chilly days, or you can sit or dine under the shade of the trees and awnings on warmer ones. Anywhere you wander, it's hard to top the spectacular views of the lake below.

The Schobers have maintained the friendly, informal atmosphere that guests have relied on since the inn's in-ception. Glancing through the guest book, you'll discover many names reap-pearing year after year—one indication of their success.

🏨 *8 doubles with bath, 2 doubles share bath, 1 double with hall bath, 2 apart-ments. Restaurant; phone, cable TV in 1 apartment; private lake beach. $63–$73, apartments $80–$140; breakfast extra. AE, MC, V. No pets. 2-night min-imum weekends. Closed Jan.–late Mar.*

House on the Hill

92 Woodbury Terrace, Waterbury 06710, tel. 203/757–9901

"Rus en urbe" ("city and country") is owner-innkeeper Marianne Vandenburgh's motto for her House on the Hill. The Latin phrase is an apt description of this fanciful B&B, which is surrounded by lush gardens in Waterbury's historic Hillside neighborhood.

The three-story, 20-room Victorian has a glorious exterior color scheme of teal, sage green, red, and ivory. It was built in 1888 by the Camp family—brass barons of this industrial Brass City—and Marianne is its third owner. The curved central staircase, the hand-carved paneling and fireplace surrounds, the built-in cabinetry, the intricate mold-ings, and the wainscoting are testaments to all three owners' respect for crafts-manship. Today, as more than a century ago, the library—with its rich mahogany, its fireplace, and its cinnamon-colored walls—is a favorite gathering spot. In warm weather the hammock on the west porch is *the* place to lounge.

When Marianne isn't outside tending to her gardens, she's inside tending to your creature comforts. An ample supply of tea, coffee, and cocoa in each room and sherry in the library are among her considerate touches. She has infused welcoming comfort in the four guest suites, which are furnished with a carefully chosen mix of antiques and memorabilia. The suite in the turret at the tip-top of the house is a favorite. Its spacious bedroom and sitting room are separated by sliding pocket doors made of the same rich oak used for the moldings, the mantel, and the floor. The fern green walls pick up the colors of the stained-glass window over the fireplace, and light pours in through windows in the eastern, western, and southern walls.

Although Waterbury's attractions (a museum, a theater, a symphony, and a ballet) and the charms of Litchfield are nearby, guests are never in a hurry to rush out each morning. They prefer to linger in the antiques-filled kitchen watching Marianne do her stuff. Breakfast may consist of fluffy pancakes made with cornmeal ground at Marianne's parent's Ohio farm, lemon French toast, or green eggs (scrambled with cheese and fresh herbs) and ham. The food, like the rest of the inn, is memorable.

🏨 *4 suites. Air-conditioning in 1 suite; cable TV, phones in all suites; VCR in 2 suites. $100–$150; full breakfast. No credit cards, no smoking. 2-night minimum weekends. Closed Dec. 15–Jan. 15.*

The Mayflower Inn

118 Woodbury Rd. (Rte. 47), Washington 06793, tel. 860/868–9466, fax 860/868–1497

Oh, to live every day as they do at the Mayflower. This picture-perfect country inn—a three-story clapboard-and-shingle beauty—is in Washington, an ever-so-perfect country village perched atop

a mound of old New England money. Perfection, however, comes with a price: Certain suites here will set you back $580 a night. Nevertheless, weekends have been booked solid since Adriana and Robert Mnuchin opened the inn in March 1992. On any given Saturday afternoon you'll find the parking lot bumper to bumper with limos and BMWs.

If you can stand that the Reynolds portrait in the parlor is a tad livelier than many of the guests (note that this is not a place for children), this opulent, if self-conscious, country inn is worth a splurge. The 28 impeccably groomed acres are replete with streams, stone walls, century-old rhododendrons, rare specimen trees, and hiking trails, not to mention a fitness center better suited to an NFL football team than a gaggle of bon vivants. And each of the 17 rooms and 8 suites, spread among the main inn, the Standish House, and the Speedwell, is decorated with fine 19th-century English and French antiques and four-poster canopy beds (with Frette linen sheets and lush featherbeds); the walls are hung with noteworthy prints and paintings and papered in Regency stripes. Sherry is, of course, always waiting on the sideboard, and the colossal mahogany-wainscoted bathrooms are marble throughout, with brass and Limoges fittings and handmade Belgian tapestries set importantly upon the floors.

If all that doesn't entice you, the mouth-watering cuisine of renowned chef Thomas Moran probably will. Although the menu changes daily, you may be tempted by such an appetizer as smoked salmon with a potato, caper, and crème fraîche salad and such an entrée as roasted duck breast on a barley, wheatberry, and vegetable risotto. If nothing else, come just to stare at this imposing compound.

🏨 *17 doubles with bath, 8 suites. Restaurant; air-conditioning, cable TV, phones, minibars in rooms; fireplaces in*

14 rooms; massages; heated pool; fitness center; yoga; game room; boutique; meeting rooms; tennis. $240–$580; breakfast extra. AE, MC, V. No smoking, no pets. 2-night minimum weekends, 3-night minimum holiday weekends.

Stonehenge

Box 667, Ridgefield 06877, tel. 203/438–6511, fax 203/438–2478

Just off busy Route 7 in Ridgefield are the 10 acres of manicured lawns, woodlands, and bright white-clapboard buildings that are part of the Stonehenge inn and restaurant. Once the proud domain of celebrated chef Albert Stockli, it is operated today by Douglas Seville, a veteran of the hotel business. The original 18th-century inn was destroyed by a fire in June 1988, and, alas, the new building lacks period charm. The new rooms, as well as those in the cottage and the guest house, are tasteful, though you won't find a period piece anywhere. Instead, Stonehenge has a plethora of Waverly and Schumacher prints, a 10-ft gilt-framed mirror above a king-size bed, the latest chic magazines, and wall-to-wall carpeting. The dining—today presided over by well-known chef Christian Bertrand—is still magnificent, and the service is impeccable, right down to the morning paper and Continental breakfast delivered to your doorstep.

🏠 *14 doubles with bath, 2 suites. Restaurant; room service; air-conditioning, cable TV, phones in rooms; minirefrigerators in suites. $120–$200; Continental breakfast. AE, MC, V. No pets.*

Tucker Hill Inn

96 Tucker Hill Rd., Middlebury 06762, tel. 203/758–8334, fax 203/598–0652

Built in 1923, this Colonial-style clapboard just down the road from the village green looks every bit the New England B&B, right down to the pineapple welcome flag flying out front. It was once a tea room at a trolley stop, but when Susan Cebelenski bought it in 1985, she applied her formal training (acquired in many classes on how to run a successful B&B) combined with the practical experience she had gained as a retailer in New York and transformed it into an inn. The result this ebullient proprietress has achieved is a pleasant inn with a few spacious rooms for guests and cozy sitting and dining areas. Two of Susan's three children and her songwriter husband have their own space elsewhere in the building. The guest rooms are attractively done with an assortment of country-style antiques and furnishings, delicate wallpapers, and floral fabrics. A full, homemade breakfast is served in the spacious dining room, and afternoon tea and coffee (and cookies!) are presented in the sitting room.

🏠 *2 doubles with bath, 2 doubles share bath. Air-conditioning in 2 rooms; ceiling fans, cable TV/VCR, terry-cloth robes in all rooms. $75–$120; full breakfast. AE, MC, V. No smoking, no pets.*

West Lane Inn

22 West La., Ridgefield 06877, tel. 203/438–7323, fax 203/438–7325

Set behind a broad expanse of carefully groomed lawn, this three-story Colonial-style mansion built in the late 1800s rises above a long columned sweep of porches. Only minutes from the center of Ridgefield and adjacent to the Inn at Ridgefield, the setting recalls a quieter time of small-town American life.

Maureen Mayer, the owner-manager, has carefully reconstructed just such an atmosphere in the 19 years she has spent converting this former summer residence into a gracious inn. The former model and New York restaurateur is equally at ease supervising the efficient staff to ensure her high standards of comfort—and daughter Deborah Prieger is fast following in her footsteps.

From the moment you step inside the rich, oak-paneled lobby and (on cold days) feel the warmth of the cozy fire in the Victorian fireplace, you begin to get that country-inn feeling. Guest rooms have well-chosen 19th-century period furnishings, and comfort is the byword; the four-poster queen-size and king-size beds, the upholstered wing chairs, and the tables and lamps all seem to fit in the oversize, high-ceiling rooms with their tall windows. Two rooms have working fireplaces that you're invited to light on chilly evenings. A carriage house out back has been converted to similarly furnished guest quarters with small kitchens. Most recently, cable TV and a personalized voice-mail system were added, to the joy of the West Lane's many business clients.

The lobby is a gathering place for guests when the weather prohibits sitting on the porches. Breakfast is served in a brightly wallpapered breakfast room directly off the lobby. There's a cozy intimacy at West Lane Inn that makes it easy to strike up a conversation with fellow guests. You can just stretch out and listen to the sound of the birds . . . or to the carillon concert from a nearby church.

🏨 *18 doubles with bath. Air-conditioning, cable TV, phones in rooms; kitchenettes in some rooms; laundry and dry cleaning available; meeting room. $125–$165; Continental breakfast, full breakfast extra. AE, DC, MC, V. No pets. 2-night minimum holiday weekends.*

The Southeastern Coast

Bee & Thistle Inn

As you head east from New Haven, the urban clutter of factories, apartment towers, and shopping malls dissipates gradually, and before long you encounter long stretches of road without a single man-made intrusion. Although some industry and large cities have developed where major streams flow into Long Island Sound, the area is mostly a string of small communities, proud of their individual attractions and their heritage.

In a bygone era venturesome Yankee merchants sent their ships from thriving ports in search of whale oil, rum, household goods, and spices. At one time New London was the second-busiest whaling port on the Atlantic, and Mystic, long famed for shipbuilding and maritime exploits, vigorously preserves that identity today. But the seafaring adventurers have mostly disappeared, and nowadays only tiny Stonington Village can claim the distinction of a commercial fishing fleet.

Although there's substantial activity in this region year-round, it is best seen and enjoyed in warm weather. In spring and summer, boats—from dinghies to yachts—get their barnacles scraped, and they dot the local waters. Pollution has been largely eliminated from the sound's formerly sullied waters, so opportunities for swimming, sunbathing, fishing, sailing, waterskiing, and even surfing abound.

Offshore exploration is a popular pastime. The Thimble Islands off the Branford coast abound with legends of pirate gold buried by the infamous Captain Kidd. And those with a scientific bent can board numerous vessels that leave Mystic and New London for supervised oceanographic explorations. Landlubbers will find substantial marine exhibits in the region's many museums and nature centers.

Browsing in stores is an inevitable activity. The coastal towns have numerous shops, some selling tacky nautical reproductions made elsewhere, others offering genuine marine artifacts and fine antiques. This gives you the chance to try to outsmart the shrewd Yankees and, once in a while, come away with a true bargain.

Places to Go, Sights to See

In Ledyard, on the Mashantucket Indian Reservation, the **Foxwoods Casino** (Rte. 2, tel. 860/885–3000 or 800/752–9244) has the state's first—and the world's largest—gambling operation. It's open daily around the clock. This surprisingly attractive, skylighted, Colonial-style compound draws more than 55,000 visitors daily to its slot machines, 3,500-seat bingo parlor, poker rooms, smoke-free gaming area, 16 restaurants, and more.

Mohegan Sun (Exit 79A off I–395, tel. 860/848–5682), which opened in October 1996 on the banks of the Thames River in Uncasville, is the state's second casino. Although smaller in scale than Foxwoods, it, too, offers all the expected gaming and entertainment options: slot machines, gaming tables, bingo, fine dining, and entertainment in the Wolf Den.

Mystic Seaport. Start with a visit to the nation's oldest *maritime museum* (tel. 860/572–0711) and check out its 17 riverfront acres before moving along to *Olde Mistick Village* (tel. 860/536–4941), a commercial but picturesque re-creation of an early 18th-century hamlet. You're right next door to the *Mystic Marinelife Aquarium* (tel. 860/536–3323), which has more than 6,000 specimens and 50 live exhibits of sea creatures.

Outlet Bound. Bargain hunters rejoice! *Clinton Crossing Premium Outlets* (Exit 63 off I–95, tel. 860/664–0700) in Clinton and *Westbrook Factory Stores*

(Exit 65 off I–95, tel. 860/399–8656) in Westbrook feature 70 and 65 stores, respectively.

U.S. Naval Submarine Base (Exit 86 off I–95, tel. 860/449–3174). Across the Thames River in Groton, you're in submarine territory, albeit friendly waters. You can board the first nuclear-powered vessel and visit the *Nautilus Submarine Force Museum* all in one day.

Beaches

Hammonasset Beach State Park (Exit 62 off I–95, tel. 203/245–2785) has a 2-mi strip of sand as well as facilities for swimming, camping, and picnicking. **Ocean Beach Park** (Ocean Ave., tel. 860/447–3031) in New London offers an Olympic-size outdoor pool with a triple water slide, a kids' pool and playground, miniature golf, a boardwalk with the usual concessions, and a picnic area—as well as swimming in the sound. **Rocky Neck State Park** (Rte. 156, Niantic, tel. 860/739–5471) is not even a mile long, but it offers one of the nicest saltwater bathing sites in the state. It also has a public bathhouse, picnic grounds and shelters, camp-grounds, and fishing facilities.

Restaurants

Almost any restaurant you walk into off the street will have the usual local favorites—chowder, lobster, clams, and the perennial fish fry. Maybe the best of the bunch is Noank's **Abbott's Lobster in the Rough** (2 mi southwest of Mystic, Exit 89 off I–95, tel. 860/536–7719), an unassuming seafood shanty that's open only from Memorial Day to Columbus Day. For fine new American cuisine, try Old Saybrook's **Aleia's** (1697 Boston Post Rd., tel. 860/399–5050). Contemporary Italian dining is what you'll find at **Bravo Bravo** (21 Main St., tel. 860/536–3228), part of the Whaler's Inn complex, in Mystic. Finally, for old-fashioned thin-crust, brick-oven-fired pizza, the **Recovery Room** (444 Ocean Ave., tel. 860/443–2619), in New London, is a top choice.

Nightlife and the Arts

In Stony Creek, a tiny village that's part of Branford, you'll find theater at the **Puppet House Theatre** (tel. 203/488–5752) from March through December. In New London, Connecticut College's **Palmer Auditorium** (tel. 860/439–2787) presents both dance and theater programs, and the **Garde Arts Center** (tel. 860/444–6766) hosts the Eastern Connecticut Symphony Orchestra, a Broadway-style theater series, innovative dance programs, and a number of well-known performers.

Reservations Services

Bed & Breakfast, Ltd. (Box 216, New Haven 06513, tel. 203/469–3260), **Covered Bridge Bed & Breakfast Reservation Service** (Box 447, Norfolk 06058, tel.

860/542–5944), **Nutmeg Bed & Breakfast Agency** (Box 1117, West Hartford 06127, tel. 860/236–6698 or 800/727–7592).

Visitor Information

Connecticut's Mystic and More (470 Bank St., Box 89, New London 06320, tel. 860/444–2206 or 800/863–6569), **Connecticut River Valley and Shoreline Visitors Council** (393 Main St., Middletown 06457, tel. 860/347–0028 or 800/486–3346).

Antiques & Accommodations

32 Main St., North Stonington 06359, tel. 860/535–1736 or 800/554–7829, fax 860/535–2613

The British accent of this 1861 Victorian B&B in the center of North Stonington is no accident. Owner-managers Thomas and Ann Gray are avowed Anglophiles who travel twice yearly to England to buy things for the house. Their background as appraisers and liquidators of antiques has stood them in good stead; the place is teeming with them.

And here's good news for guests: Some of what you see is for sale. The Grays decided to combine their multiple interests by running a small, elegantly decorated hostelry that doubles as an antiques shop. Do you like that pair of Ponty Pool sconces with the unusual George III seals? That painted-pine 19th-century corner cupboard? How about the Massachusetts Sheraton four-poster in Timothy's Room? It could be yours . . . for a price.

The rooms are furnished, it should be noted, with *livable* antiques. In the ground-floor Jeni's Room there are a small library, a working fireplace, and an antique chandelier over the bed. The bridal suite is called Susan's Room after one of the first brides to nest here. All the rooms are filled with bright Victorian touches with fresh as well as dried flower arrangements and gently scented candles everywhere. A multicourse candlelight breakfast using sterling silver, crystal, and bone china is served to those who stay in the main house guest rooms or the suites in the adjacent 1820 Colonial. Dishes might include crabmeat Benedict, a salmon and aquavit omelet, or cantaloupe and honeydew soup, all garnished with fresh flowers in season.

The front parlor is a pleasant place to relax and have tea; in warm weather, however, you might prefer the stone terrace out front, shaded by a flowering crabapple tree. You might also stroll through the fragrant English and herb gardens. As you amble in the early morning sun, you may savor the memory of breakfast, or let your thoughts drift to the turned-down bedclothes and the decanter of cream sherry awaiting you at the end of the day.

▦ *3 doubles with bath, 2 multibedroom suites. Air-conditioning, cable TV in rooms; canoes; bicycles; box lunches available. $169–$225; full breakfast. D, MC, V. No smoking.*

Bee & Thistle Inn

100 Old Lyme St., Old Lyme 06371, tel. 860/434–1667 or 800/622–4946, fax 860/434–3402

On a long, wide avenue in the Old Lyme historic district, behind a weathered stone wall, is a two-story 1756 Colonial house that has evolved gracefully into the Bee & Thistle Inn. Set on 5½ acres along the Lieutenant River, which joins the Connecticut to flow into Long Island Sound, the inn's broad lawns, towering trees, formal flower garden, and herbaceous borders will charm you.

In the 14 years since Penny and Bob Nelson left behind the corporate world and academia in New York, they have realized a family dream here. A complete turnaround in their lifestyle occurred when they decided to become innkeepers while their two children were in the last years of school. But so successful were they and such was the lure of this special place that both kids now work here: son Jeff (a former line chef at Boston's Ritz-Carlton) in the kitchen and daughter Lori out front greeting, seating, and helping guests settle in. (Given the inn's romantic appeal, however, it's best to leave *your* children at home.)

Restoration has taken priority over renovation—which they have done only when comfort was at stake—and the result is the re-creation of a Colonial ambience in the best sense. The scale of rooms throughout is deliberately small and inviting, with fireplaces in the downstairs parlors and dining rooms and light and airy curtains at the multipaned guest room windows. Almost all rooms have canopy or four-poster beds, with old quilts and afghans providing warmth when needed. Little touches change with the seasons—hanging on each door might be tiny ribboned straw hats or sprigs of evergreen or holly. No slave to Colonial New England style, Penny brings to the rooms touches of Williamsburg and even Victoriana, with such oddities as a wing chair our Puritan forebears surely wouldn't recognize.

Breakfast can be brought to your room before or after a morning soak in an herbal bath (scented soap provided). And downstairs you might encounter a harpist one evening or take high tea late some winter afternoon. In the restaurant a romantic atmosphere is created by working fireplaces and candlelight that, coupled with high-class cuisine, make for a memorable evening.

🏠 *11 doubles with bath, cottage with bath. Restaurant; air-conditioning, phones in rooms; cable TV in cottage. $75–$155, cottage $210; breakfast extra with exception of cottage. AE, DC, MC, V. No smoking, no pets. Closed 2 wks in Jan.*

Captain Stannard House

138 S. Main St., Westbrook 06498, tel. 860/399-4634

On South Main Street in Westbrook, the two-story clapboard house with a cupola on its roof looks like the sea captain's house that it was in the 19th century. Today it holds sway as a B&B and antiques shop in the hands of Verner Mettin and his wife, Lee Willman, who have owned it since 1990. They have refurbished the rooms and the grounds entirely. Breakfast, which might include orange-nut pancakes, is served in the large bright dining room with its elegant fireplace, baby grand piano, and decorative antiques. The quaint library, which has cable TV, doubles as a lounge where drinks are served. The common area has a woodstove, a pool table, a chess set, darts, and a wall of books; you'll also find antiques and local crafts for sale.

"The theme is 'casual,'" says the laid-back Mettin. "I've been traveling for 25 years myself, and here I intend to take the hassle out of traveling." (Note, though, that however casual this inn may be, it's not suitable for children.) The beach is but a block away; the Pilots Point Marina is nearby, too. Whatever you need to borrow—picnic basket, lawn chair, cooler—you need only ask for.

🏠 *6 doubles with bath. Air-conditioning, common refrigerator, bicycles, croquet set. $95; full breakfast. MC, V. No smoking, no pets. 2-night minimum weekends. Closed Jan.–Mar.*

Harbour Inne & Cottage

15 Edgemont St., Mystic 06355, tel. 860/572-9253

On a small inlet of the Mystic River, one block from the train station, you'll find a simple 1950s-style bungalow where Charley Lecouras, Jr., welcomes overnight guests. With its neatly clipped lawn surrounded on three sides by water, this location is ideal for spotting herons, loons, and more common waterfowl. Charley is at home most evenings, and various handymen and caretakers are around throughout the day. The rustic cedar-paneled bedrooms are fairly small and have simple, modern maple furniture. The decor leans heavily toward a nautical theme. Some rooms lack good bedside lamps and may be a bit cramped, but there's a cozy lounge with an antique piano and a fireplace (and plenty of wood). The recently redone kitchen is for guests. A three-room cottage next door has its own kitchen, fireplace in the bedroom, hot tub on the deck, and can sleep up to six.

▥ 5 doubles with bath, 3-room cottage. Air-conditioning, cable TV in rooms; gazebo by water; gas grill; picnic facilities. $95–$135, cottage $200–$250; no breakfast. No credit cards. 2-night minimum weekends Memorial Day–late Oct.

Lasbury's Guest House

41 Orchard St., Stonington 06378, tel. 860/535-2681

Strolling (the preferred method of local locomotion) down a side street in compact Stonington Village, you'll pass the big brick schoolhouse that has "gone condo" on your way to the Orchard Street residence of mother and daughter, Mae and Jayne Lasbury. From this small frame house built in 1860, they're pleased to report that five generations of Lasburys walked to that school. They're just as pleased to show you to their little red guest house—across a tiny garden from the main house—where they offer trim, quiet lodgings year-round. The guest rooms, best suited to couples or those traveling with older children, overlook a salt marsh that drifts off to Long Island Sound. They have no-nonsense traditional-style furniture, curtains and bedcoverings in light colors, and framed prints announcing such events as the annual Stonington Village Fair. This is not the most lavish of inns, but it is the only one in this delightful village.

▥ 3 doubles share 2 baths. Air-conditioning in 2 rooms; cable TV, minirefrigerators in all rooms. $85; no breakfast. No credit cards. No pets. 2-night minimum summer and holiday weekends.

Old Lyme Inn

Box 787, 85 Lyme St., Old Lyme 06371, tel. 860/434-2600, fax 860/434-5352

Less than a mile from exit 70 off I-95 you'll come to a bend in the road and a gray-clapboard 1850s farmhouse with crisp blue shutters that is the center-piece of the Old Lyme Inn. Diana Field Atwood, the innkeeper of more than 20 years, has transformed what was once a rundown Italian restaurant into a warm, attractive dining and lodging establishment in the heart of the historic district. Behind the ornate iron fence, the tree-shaded lawn, and the banistered front porch, you'll find attractive, spacious guest rooms impeccably decorated with carefully selected antiques and contemporary furnishings. When she isn't busy working for the local art academy or the Connecticut River Museum, Diana is lifting pot lids in the kitchen for whiffs of the gourmet treats served by her chef in the always-busy dining rooms. She also collects local art, some of which is displayed in the cozy ground-floor common rooms.

▥ 5 doubles with bath, 8 suites. Restaurant; air-conditioning, cable TV, phones in rooms; cable TV, working fireplace in library. $109–$158; Continental breakfast. AE, D, DC, MC, V. Closed Jan. 1–15.

The Palmer Inn

25 Church St. (2 mi southwest of Mystic, exit 89 off I-95), Noank 06340, tel. 860/572-9000

On a side street in the tiny fishing village of Noank, the Palmer Inn rises majestically behind tall hedges that permit just a glimpse of its tall, white Corinthian columns. This imposing southern Colonial-style house was erected in 1907 by a local shipbuilder as an exact copy of a Knoxville mansion. His own artisans were responsible for the exquisite interior woodwork. Patricia White, the owner-innkeeper (who also makes the jams, muffins, breads, and granola served at breakfast), proudly points out unusual design features, such as the original tilelike Lincrusta Walton wallpaper along the main stairway, the three museum-quality grandfather clocks in the hallways, and the inn's 11 stained-glass windows. Followed by Arthur and Dickens, her dachshunds, she'll show you the spacious bedrooms, which are furnished with family heirlooms and antiques, including an ornate Eastlake bed and an original Morris chair. They're complemented by Schumacher wallpapers that suit the late-Victorian period. The Balcony Room on the third floor has a fine view of Long Island Sound. Downstairs, the impressive Victorian parlor is made cozy by a glowing fire. Breakfast is served here at an intricately carved dining room table set with English china, silver, and linens.

🏠 *6 doubles with bath. Air-conditioning in rooms. $115–$215; hearty Continental breakfast. AE, D, MC, V. No smoking, no pets. Children must be old enough to have their own room. 2-night minimum weekends July–Oct.*

Randall's Ordinary

Rte. 2, Box 243, North Stonington 06359, tel. 860/599–4540, fax 860/599–3308

As you leave the Westerly–Norwich Road (Route 2) and continue up the short drive to this enclave of centuries-old weathered frame buildings on 27 wooded acres, you could easily be a Colonial traveler seeking an inn. In the 17th century each town approved one such establishment through an ordinance, giving rise to the designation *ordinary*. The original 1685 building now houses a restaurant widely celebrated for its open-hearth cooking (be sure to try the sautéed Nantucket sea scallops) and for its three primitively furnished guest rooms upstairs.

Across the drive is the 1819 Jacob Terpenning Barn, moved from upstate New York and converted to lodgings in 1989, with 12 rooms on three floors. Period authenticity is achieved through the use of canopy and four-poster beds, simple furniture, and a smattering of antiques. However, the largely bare floors and walls also create a spartan look that nonantiquarians might feel could use some warming up. The tavern atmosphere of the restaurant in the main

house does a lot to fill that gap. So does the dramatic multilevel Silo Suite with its rustic queen-size birch Adirondack bed, weathered barn doors as wall art, fireplace, skylighted cathedral ceiling, and whirlpool-for-two in a domed loft that looks out over the treetops.

🏠 *14 doubles with bath, 1 suite. Air-conditioning, whirlpool baths in rooms; cable TV, phones in barn rooms. $115, suite $195; Continental breakfast. AE, MC, V. No pets. 2-night minimum holiday weekends.*

Steamboat Inn

73 Steamboat Wharf, Mystic 06355, tel. 860/536–8300

Location, location, location—it's hard to top that of this posh inn settled dockside just a foot from the Mystic River in the heart of downtown Mystic. Each of the rooms in the yellow clapboard built in the early 1800s is named after a famous Mystic ship from the long-ago-and-faraway days of schooners: *Annie Wilcox, Ariadne, Marie Gilbert, Early Dawn*—their photos can be seen around the inn. Furnished with fine antiques and reproductions, all but one of the spacious rooms have superb water views. Peek your head outside the second-story window of *Summer Girl*, and you have a fine view of not only the Mystic drawbridge but the *Argia* cruise ship docked beneath your window. *Harmony* has a king-size bed whose headboard is fashioned from antique church doors, a wet bar, and a *double* whirlpool tub. Before you head out for a busy day downtown, a spread of home-baked muffins, fresh fruits, bagels, and granola is laid out for your pleasure in the crisp black-and-white-tiled common room. It is here, too, that you may partake of a touch of sherry late in the afternoon.

🏠 *10 doubles with bath. Air-conditioning, cable TV, phones, whirlpool baths in rooms; fireplaces in 6 rooms; wet bars, minirefrigerators in 4 rooms. $175–$275; Continental-plus*

breakfast. AE, D, MC, V. No smoking,
no pets. 2-night minimum weekends.

Stonecroft

*515 Pumpkin Hill Rd., Ledyard 06339,
tel. 860/572-0771, fax 860/572-9161*

Owners Joan and Lyn Egy opened this
B&B—set in a historic Georgian Colonial
on 6½ acres of meadows, woodlands, and
rambling stone walls—to create a romantic retreat for couples looking to "re-
connect." It is, indeed, a beautiful place
to do so. There are countless ways and
places to relax at Stonecroft: by the 9-ft-
wide Rumford fireplace in the Great
Room, curled up with a good book in the
Snuggery (once the house's borning
room), via a rousing game of croquet on
the lawn, stretched out on a hammock in
the meadow, or even joining others for
Joan's four-course breakfast by candlelight. Of course, Stonecroft's four rooms
are also designed for "letting go," as Joan
likes to say. Downstairs, the Buttery,
which dates from 1740 and is the inn's
oldest room, has a white iron-and-brass
queen-size bed as its centerpiece; it also
has a private terrace and is wheelchair
accessible. A main staircase, adorned
with a vibrant mural of hot-air balloons,
leads to three rooms on the second floor,
all with fireplaces. The Stonecroft Room,
furnished with spiffy tiger-maple reproductions, also has a wraparound mural
depicting Stonecroft in the 19th century
(look for the Beatles cloaked in turn-of-
the-century garb entertaining on the
lower lawn).

🏠 *4 doubles with bath. Air-conditioning
in rooms; bicycles, horseshoes, darts;
massages on request. $130–$170; full
breakfast. AE, MC, V. No smoking, no
pets. 2-night minimum weekends.*

Talcott House

*161 Seaside Ave., Box 1016, Westbrook
06498, tel. 203/399-5020*

You can't miss the scent of salt air when
you pull up to this 1890 cedar-shingle

beach cottage, a popular shoreline B&B
for couples and families with teens.
Owner Jim Fitzpatrick has removed all
trace of clutter and has kept furnishings
simple, though of the highest quality.
The highly polished floor in the main
salon reflects the light that streams in
the front windows down its 50-ft length,
from one fireplace to another at the opposite end. A ground-floor guest room
has its own screened brick-floor patio
with a view of the sound. The remainder
of the guest rooms, all upstairs, have
similarly shiny floors with an assortment
of attractive carpets, brass beds, hobnail spreads, and walls painted in pale
colors. All these rooms have uninter-
rupted views of the ocean. Jim, who also
owns and operates the Cuckoo's Nest, a
Mexican restaurant in Old Saybrook,
and innkeeper Donald Correll call breakfast "Continental plus." You can count on
an emphasis on the "plus"—homemade
muffins, fresh fruit, bacon and eggs, and
baked French toast.

🏠 *4 doubles with bath. $125–$135; Continental-plus breakfast. MC, V. No
smoking, no pets. 2-night minimum
weekends, July–Aug.*

Tidewater Inn

*949 Boston Post Rd., Madison 06443, tel.
203/245-8457, fax 203/318-0265*

In the 1800s the Boston Post Road was
a mere dirt path, and the building that
now houses the Tidewater Inn was a
stagecoach stop. Today, as anyone who
has traveled through Connecticut
knows, the heavily commercialized
Boston Post Road (Route 1) is far from
a path. Luckily, the Tidewater is perched
around one of its quieter corners and
just on the edge of delightfully old-fashioned downtown Madison.

All of the nine rooms here are designed
for relaxation and are furnished with a
comforting mix of antiques, reproductions, and estate furniture with a touch
of Asian influence. (Indeed, because of all
the fine furnishings here, it's best to

leave your wee ones home.) The Madison Room has a king-size four-poster bed as well as a sitting area with a love seat and wing-backed chair. Two rooms have wood-burning fireplaces, and one, in the adjacent Curtis Cottage, has a double whirlpool bath. Innkeepers Jean Foy and Rich Evans take care of the details—a refrigerator for your use; a butler's basket should you forget your toothbrush, your blow dryer, or your aspirin; and, best of all, passes to the town beaches.

Breakfast, served beside the sitting room's sunny bay window, includes fresh fruit, home-baked goods, and entrées such as coconut French toast. Afternoon tea or, on the weekends, wine from local Chamard Vineyard is often shared by the sitting-room fire or beneath an umbrella in the lush English gardens.

🏨 *9 doubles with bath. Air-conditioning, cable TV, phones, terry-cloth robes in rooms; VCR in 2 rooms. $100–$160; full breakfast. AE, MC, V. No smoking, no pets. 2-night minimum weekends July–Aug. and holidays.*

Connecticut River Valley

Riverwind

As the Connecticut River flows south from the state capital
to Long Island Sound, it looks beyond its banks at a broad
variety of landscapes, from the high-rise urban environment
of Hartford to the Colonial seaports at the mouth of the river.
This kaleidoscope is part of the region's allure—if you're not
happy where you are at a given moment, you don't have to go
far for a change. There are the political, commercial, and
cultural vibrancy of Hartford at one end of the spectrum and
the relaxed charm and small-town coziness of Ivoryton at the
other; the exhaust fumes of the urban end of the road contrast
with the dust of the ages settling on tree-shaded streets at its
rural opposite.

And then, of course, there's the river itself. For many years
this was a major commercial artery, with goods floating up
and down its navigable waters. Industry grew up along the
shorelines and poured its waste into this too-convenient
source of disposal. The price of that shortsightedness is being
paid today, but with the rise in ecological consciousness, the
efforts to improve the quality of this beautiful waterway are
seeing significant gains. Varieties of marine life that were
virtually extinct are starting to reappear in abundance—

much to the delight of the fishing enthusiasts, who are also finding their way back.

For a long time the resort business that had thrived in earlier decades declined, and once-quaint tourist shops began to look dated and dilapidated. But there has been a movement toward renovation, and some establishments are once again appealing, with fresh coats of paint and new variations on their cutesy names. This renewal appears to have paid off by attracting a new crop of visitors to the area.

Connecticut still has one of the highest percentages of forest and undeveloped land in the country. You don't have to go many miles from either side of the river to find unspoiled woodland. State parks and nature preserves welcome all who respect the environment and who will leave it much as it has been for centuries.

Places to Go, Sights to See

Gillette Castle State Park (Off Rte. 82, East Haddam, tel. 860/526–2336). In 1919 the actor William Gillette, who made his fortune on stage bringing the character of Sherlock Holmes to life, moved into this fieldstone hilltop mansion, which overlooks the river and is modeled after the medieval castles of the Rhineland. He lived here until his death, when the property was bequeathed to the state. The 200-acre grounds (ideal for hiking and picnicking) and the castle are open from Memorial Day through mid-December. The Victorian Christmas decoration of the house is spectacular.

Goodspeed Opera House (Rte. 82, East Haddam, tel. 860/873–8668). Right on the river, this celebrated Victorian gingerbread was built in 1876 by a wealthy merchant as a home for his mercantile and theatrical interests. It was where such Broadway hits as *Annie* and *Man of La Mancha* were first staged, and today it is the setting for acclaimed revivals of vintage musicals as well as premieres.

Mark Twain House (351 Farmington Ave., Hartford, tel. 860/493–6411) and **Harriet Beecher Stowe House** (71 Forest St., Hartford, tel. 860/525–9317). A neatly trimmed lawn separates these two historic Hartford homes. At the Twain property the esteemed author built his Victorian mansion in 1874. During his residency he published seven major novels, including *Tom Sawyer, Huckleberry Finn,* and *The Prince and the Pauper.* Personal memorabilia and original furnishings are on display. The Stowe House, erected in 1871, stands as a tribute to the author of one of 19th-century America's most popular novels, *Uncle Tom's Cabin.* Inside are Stowe's personal writing table and effects, several of her paintings, a period pinewood kitchen, and a terrarium of native mosses and wildflowers.

Wadsworth Atheneum (600 Main St., Hartford, tel.860/278–2670). This, the first public art museum in the country, has more than 50,000 works spanning 5,000 years, including paintings from the Hudson River school (it's the largest such collection in the country), the impressionists, and 20th-century painters. The museum also mounts changing exhibits of contemporary art and has an estimable collection of Pilgrim-era furnishings. The Fleet Gallery of African-American Art, opened in 1993, is one of the nation's best collections.

Outdoor Activities and Sports

If you don't want to hoist your own sail or pilot your own vessel, you can still enjoy a day or evening on the river aboard a number of cruise ships that ply these waters. The **Valley Railroad** offers 90-minute-long riverboat voyages aboard the *Becky Thatcher* or *Silver Star,* leaving from Deep River (tel. 860/526–4954). Several **Camelot** cruises (tel. 860/345–8591) leave the dock at Haddam.

Restaurants

In Hartford a couple great choices are **Max Downtown** (185 Asylun St., tel. 860/522–2530), for a chic atmosphere and cosmopolitan eats, and **Peppercorns Grill** (357 Main St., tel. 860/547–1714), a funky bistro that's usually packed with well-heeled yuppies. The best food northwest of the city is easily that served at **Ann Howard's Apricots** (1593 Farmington Ave., Farmington, tel. 860/673–5903), whose dining room looks over gardens and toward the Farmington River. Tiny Chester, just north of East Haddam, has several fine eateries including the exquisite **Restaurant du Village** (59 Main St., tel. 860/526–5301), renowned for nonpareil French cuisine, and **Fiddler's** (4 Water St., tel. 860/526–3210), one of the state's better inland fish houses. Finally, the longtime favorite Fine Bouche was reincarnated in 1994 as **Steve's Centerbrook Cafe** (Exit 3 off Rte. 9, Centerbrook, tel. 860/767–1277), which now specializes in nouvelle pasta and seafood dishes.

Nightlife and the Arts

The performing arts have always been a mainstay all along the river and continue to draw fans year-round. In Hartford **The Bushnell** theater (tel. 860/246–6807) brings in touring attractions, while the Tony Award–winning **Hartford Stage Company** (tel. 860/527–5151) generates its own hits. The Goodspeed Opera House operates on a smaller scale with new works at the **Norma Terris Theatre** in Chester (tel. 860/873–8668), and the **Ivoryton Playhouse** (tel. 860/767–8348) continues its longstanding success with the River Rep during the summer season.

Reservation Services

Bed & Breakfast, Ltd. (Box 216, New Haven 06513, tel. 203/469–3260), **Covered Bridge Bed & Breakfast Reservation Service** (Box 447, Norfolk 06058, tel. 860/542–5944), **Nutmeg Bed & Breakfast Agency** (Box 1117, West Hartford 06127, tel. 860/236–6698 or 800/727–7592).

Visitor Information

Connecticut River Valley and Shoreline Visitors Council (393 Main St., Middletown 06457, tel. 860/347–0028 or 800/486–3346), **Greater Hartford Tourism District** (234 Murphy Rd., Hartford 06114, tel. 860/244–8181 or 800/793–4480).

The Barney House

11 Mountain Spring Rd., Farmington 06032, tel. 860/674–2796, fax 860/677–7259

Around the corner from the busiest intersection in Farmington you'll find a peaceful suburban street and the peach and white Barney House. Built in 1832, the Georgian mansion and its 4½ acres are owned and operated by the University of Connecticut Foundation, which runs a year-round conference center on the premises. Happily for voyagers to these parts, it also accepts overnight guests by reservation. The seven large guest rooms on the two upper floors are furnished chiefly with antiques. Some have Asian carpets, some have area rugs, and some have wall-to-wall carpeting. All have ornately papered walls, lead-glass bookcases, fetching bed quilts, and substantial bathrooms with modern plumbing. A refrigerator and coffee setup are available for guests in the Morning Room on the second-floor landing, where breakfast is served. You're invited to enjoy the garden and tennis court, as well as the cozy library with a fireplace on the first floor when it's not being used for conferences.

🏠 *7 doubles with bath. Air-conditioning, cable TV, phones in rooms; meeting rooms; tennis court. $89; Continental breakfast. AE, MC, V. No smoking, no pets.*

Bishopsgate Inn

Box 290, Goodspeed Landing, East Haddam 06423, tel. 860/873–1677

To reach the 1818 Federal-style Bishopsgate Inn, just follow the Norwich Road up around the bend from the landmark Goodspeed Opera House. Here your hosts, the Kagel family, will give you a warm welcome, including a cold drink on a hot day (or a hot one on a cold day), as well as plenty of suggestions on what to see and do. Since taking over the inn in 1995, the Kagels—Lisa and Colin, Jr.,

Jane and Colin, Sr.—have added their own special touches. Most impressive are the pencil-post beds (with fluffy feather-filled mattresses on top). Early American reproductions, family antiques, chenille spreads, and crisp curtains make all rooms cozy and inviting. The downstairs keeping room is an ideal spot to munch peanuts by the fire, although four of the five rooms do have their own fireplaces by which you can arrange to be served private dinners. The Director's Suite has its own sauna. (Note that this inn is not suitable for young children.)

🏠 *5 doubles with bath, 1 suite. Air-conditioning in rooms; picnic and box lunches available. $95–$115, suite $140; full breakfast. MC, V. No smoking, no pets. 2-night minimum holidays and some weekends.*

Chimney Crest Manor

5 Founders Dr., Bristol 06010, tel. 860/582–4219, fax 860/584–5903

This impressive 32-room Tudor-style mansion (circa 1930) in Bristol's Federal Hill District is just 20 minutes west of Hartford. Folks have been walking through the arched entrance and 40-ft-long arcade of the manor for 13 years now as the guests of owners-innkeepers Dante (Dan) and Cynthia Cimadamore. Whether you choose to relax in the cherry-paneled library, the bright Spanish-tiled sunroom, or by one of a pair of fireplaces in the salon, with its rich oak paneling and ornate plaster ceilings, Dan and Cynthia will see to your comfort.

All the guest rooms have spectacular views of the Farmington Valley, and two of the suites have fireplaces. The 40-ft-long Garden Suite, in what was once the mansion's ballroom, has gleaming hardwood floors, a fireplace, a queen-size canopy bed, its own kitchen, and tiled walls with a dazzling sunflower motif. Attention, romantics (and this *is* a place built more for romance than for family vacations): The Manor View Suite has a

Thermo-Spa. Breakfast (look for Dan's famed yogurt pancakes or Cynthia's yummy strawberry bread) is served using fine china and crystal in the formal dining room or, more casually, on the grand fieldstone patio.

▦ *2 doubles with bath, 4 suites. Air-conditioning, cable TV, terry-cloth robes, homemade cookies, fresh fruit, coffee/tea in rooms; turn-down service; hot-air ballooning. $80–$165; full breakfast. MC, V. No smoking, no pets. 2-night minimum Sept. 15–late Oct.*

Copper Beech Inn

46 Main St., Ivoryton 06442, tel. 860/767–0330, fax 860/767–7840

Picture a rambling Victorian country cottage—with a carriage barn and terraced gardens—set behind oak and beech trees on 7 acres near a river. You've just conjured up the Copper Beech Inn. Built in the 1880s as a residence for the ivory importer A. W. Comstock, the building is now a dining and lodging haven in the quintessential Connecticut River valley town of Ivoryton.

The current innkeepers, Eldon and Sally Senner, took over in 1988 and have made their mark. The four rooms in the main house have 19th-century artwork, antique furniture, and bric-a-brac that all contribute to the warm, traditional ambience. Spacious Room 1, which once belonged to the lady of the house, has two bay windows, a love seat, a chaise longue, and a king-size bed with a pale blue canopy.

The renovated carriage house has nine spacious guest rooms with cathedral ceilings and exposed beams. Although these rooms are essentially modern, the country theme of the main building is maintained in the furnishings, antique odds and ends, floral wall coverings, and botanical prints. The contemporary bathrooms here have large whirlpool tubs. With the combination of old and new, indoors and out, you truly feel as if you're in a country retreat.

At one time the ground floor of the main house was full of the endless reception rooms so beloved by the Victorians. The larger rooms have been converted to a series of dining areas that are elegant and romantic, particularly in the evening when candlelight is reflected on sparkling crystal and gleaming silver. The hearty French country cuisine is complemented by a wine list with a stellar selection of French and American vintages. In 1993 a Victorian-style solarium was added to the main house—it's now the perfect spot to sip evening cocktails before the collection of neatly framed Audubon prints.

You won't find anything stressful here. The beautiful grounds, comfortable guest rooms, abundant lounge space, lack of young guests (children under 10 are best left home), and welcoming dining rooms may well make your quest for a quiet country inn end at the Copper Beech.

▦ *13 doubles with bath. Restaurant; air-conditioning, phones in rooms; cable TV, decks in carriage-house rooms. $105–$175; Continental breakfast buffet. AE, DC, MC, V. No smoking, no pets. 2-night minimum weekends.*

Griswold Inn

36 Main St., Essex 06426, tel. 860/767–1776, fax 860/767–0481

Stretching its 11-window length along Main Street, the Griswold Inn (known affectionately as "The Gris") in Essex claims to be America's oldest inn. Who's going to argue? Everywhere you look there's a testament to its heritage. More than two centuries of catering to changing tastes has resulted in a kaleidoscope of decor—some Colonial, a touch of Federal, a little Victorian, and just as much modern as is necessary for present-day comfort. Guest rooms, with their candlewick spreads and muslin curtains, retain their ancient configurations and have sloping floors, but all also have air-conditioning and phones. (Although they don't have radios, they do have piped-in music—just another quirk to add to the list.) Still, the only TV you'll find is in the lounge of the upstart 1790 Hayden House.

The Colonial-style dining rooms here (among them the Covered Bridge Room, constructed from a bridge that was dismantled and moved here from New Hampshire) draw visitors from all over and offer an enormous variety of both traditional country-style and gourmet dishes (try the famous 1776 sausages, which come with sauerkraut and German potato salad, or the risotto croquettes). The Tap Room, built in 1738 as a schoolhouse, is ideal for after-dinner drinks. A potbelly stove keeps things cozy, an antique popcorn machine provides as much of the stuff as you can eat, and there's nightly entertainment. On Sunday, the English Hunt Breakfast—a feast of muffins, eggs, fresh cod, creamed chipped beef, and smoked bacon—is not to be missed.

🏨 *18 doubles with bath, 12 suites. Restaurant. $90–$185; Continental breakfast. AE, MC, V. No smoking, no pets.*

Riverwind

209 Main St., Deep River 06417, tel. 860/526-2014

As you approach busy downtown Deep River, you can't miss the rose-beige clapboard building with the ivory gingerbread trim. At the Riverwind, the innkeepers in residence, Barbara Barlow and Bob Bucknall, welcome you with a cup of something soothing. Barbara came north from Virginia, where she taught school for a number of years and fell in love with the Connecticut River valley. When she found this Victorian, fallen sadly into disrepair, her preservationist instincts sensed a challenge. The process involved Bob, a local builder, who saw a different challenge, which he met by wooing and winning her. Barbara, who's also a justice of the peace, has filled the house with dozens of romantic touches—it may be enough to inspire marriage or at least a renewal of vows.

New England charm and Southern hospitality make a stay here comfortable, indeed. Throughout the house you'll find countless carefully placed antiques and bibelots ("I have a collection of collections," says Barbara) and such thoughtful touches as a decanter of sherry (help yourself) in the parlor—one of eight inviting common rooms, four of which have fireplaces.

Each guest room has a theme, and all have antique furnishings, collectibles, and touches of stenciling. (Note that because of all the antiques, Riverwind is not suitable for children.) In one room you'll find a country pine bed and a painted headboard; in another there's a carved oak bed; and in still another, an 18th-century bird's-eye-maple four-poster with a canopy. The bathrooms have modern plumbing, but there's a beautiful Victorian claw-foot tub in the Barn Rose Room. In the spectacular Champagne and Roses Room, soft pinks, blues, and roses enhance a fabric-draped queen-size bed that's surrounded by a vanity desk, a carved armoire, and blush-color wing chairs. You might drink the champagne that comes with this room on its private balcony.

In the 18th-century-style keeping room that was added onto the original building just a few years ago, there's a huge stone cooking fireplace, where hot cider and rum are mulled all winter. Close by, Barbara serves a hearty country breakfast, featuring Smithfield ham, her own baked goods, and several casseroles. Freshly brewed tea and coffee and home-baked cookies are always on hand, and in the front parlor a piano is ready for those inclined to play. Such touches lift Riverwind into the realm of the extraordinary.

🏨 *7 doubles with bath (1 is hall bath), 1 suite. Air-conditioning and terry-cloth robes in rooms. $95–$165; full breakfast. AE, MC, V. No pets. 2-night minimum weekends Apr. 15–Jan. 2.*

Simsbury 1820 House

731 Hopmeadow St., Simsbury 06070, tel. 860/658–7658 or 800/879–1820, fax 860/651–0724

Perched on a hillside above the main road through Simsbury is a classic country inn—a two-story brick mansion built in 1820, with an 1890 addition on its west side. The property had ended up in the hands of the town, which didn't know what to do with it. In 1985 it was turned over to Simsbury House Associates, which rescued it from decay, restored it, and began to operate it as a country inn and restaurant.

In just a few years, the associates wrought a remarkable, wonderful change. The Brighenti family, which purchased the inn in 1997 and which owns three other area lodgings, is working hard to continue the associates' tradition of excellence. The restaurant has won praise from leading food critics; the romantic candlelight setting elicits almost as much applause as the victuals.

Guest rooms have a judicious mix of antiques and modern furnishings. Each of the 18 rooms and 2 junior suites in the main house has its special feature—a decorative fireplace or balcony, a patio, a wet bar, a dormer with a cozy window seat. The complementary use of rich colors—maroon, yellow, blue, green, and pink—and patterns creates a restful atmosphere.

Under the porte cochere and across the parking lot is the old carriage house, which now houses 11 rooms and the split-level Executive Suite, with its private patio and entrance and its Jacuzzi. The formal taupe and green decor of the rooms here is offset by touches of whimsy, including well-chosen horse prints on some bedcoverings and curtains. Most rooms have imported English four-poster beds, but in one, old barn doors are used as a combination room divider and king-size headboard. It works.

🏨 *29 doubles with bath, 3 suites. Restaurant; air-conditioning, cable TV, phones in rooms. $119–$179; Continental breakfast. AE, D, DC, MC, V. Pets allowed in 1 room of carriage house.*

The Northwest Corner

Manor House

Much to the delight of its year-round inhabitants, the northwest corner of Connecticut has never been a major transportation hub. A few well-traveled state roads—routes 7, 8, and 44—cut through the rising and falling terrain, but major interstate highways skirt the area. Even so, this corner has long been a mecca for weekend émigrés from the big cities of Boston and New York, though an increasing number are drifting in from Hartford and Fairfield County.

The region's combination of large towns and small villages is spaced far enough apart to offer broad views of a commanding landscape, and the climate is generally more severe than elsewhere in the state. The foothills of the Berkshires, with Canaan Mountain dominating the western border, present just enough of a rise to challenge hikers, intermediate skiers, and campers, who flock here seasonally.

In the active summer season, the quiet hamlets of Falls Village and Norfolk come alive with famous chamber-music festivals, and Tanglewood and other cultural meccas across the border in Massachusetts draw lovers of the performing arts. Swimming, sailing, and canoeing are popular activities on mountain lakes and ponds. The Housatonic River, which wends its way from north to south, attracts avid anglers, starting with the trout season in mid-April.

Historic homes and a few small museums are scattered throughout the region, and virtually every town has a historical society that welcomes visitors and can point out some select sights—from the fountain designed by famed architect Stanford White at the southern corner of Norfolk's village green to the factory in Lakeville where the famous Holley pocketknives were made. Many of the numerous 18th- and 19th-century houses are open to the public.

Occasional special events break the general air of calm that predominates. Canaan's Railroad Days, Winsted's Laurel Festival, and the Goshen and Riverton fairs offer a glimpse of small-town America that manages not only to survive locally but sometimes to prevail.

Places to Go, Sights to See

Ellen Battell Stoeckel Estate (Rte. 44, Norfolk Green, tel. 860/542–3000). For more than 50 years, these splendid grounds in Norfolk have been the home of the Yale School of Music and the Norfolk Chamber Music Festival. World-renowned artists and ensembles perform Friday and Saturday evenings June through August at the 900-seat Music Shed. Students perform Thursday evening and Saturday morning. The festival also presents its Indian Summer series in October.

Haystack Mountain, Dennis Hill, and **Mt. Tom.** Haystack Mountain (1,716 ft) and Dennis Hill (1,627 ft), to the north and south of Route 272 as it cuts through Norfolk, offer panoramic views of Vermont as well as the Long Island Sound. You can drive right to the top of the latter and all but the last ½ mi of the former. Adjacent to Dennis Hill, *Hillside Gardens* (tel. 860/542–5345) is one of the foremost nurseries and perennial gardens in the Northeast. You have to hike a mile to the top of Mt. Tom (1,325 ft), on Route 202 in Litchfield, but afterward you can swim in the lake that's part of the surrounding state park.

Sharon Audubon Center (325 Cornwall Bridge Rd., Sharon, tel. 860/364–0520). Not just for the birds, this more than 700-acre sanctuary has several well-marked hiking trails as well as a building housing natural-history displays, a gift shop, a bookstore, and the Children's Discovery Room.

Winchester Center. In this tiny hamlet, 18th- and 19th-century buildings surround a village green and broad pasture that stretches toward the distant hills. Right next to the white fluted columns of the Congregational church is the unique *Kerosene Lamp Museum* (Rte. 263, tel. 860/379–2612) with its impressive collection of more than 500 hanging and standing lamps dating from 1852 to 1880.

Outdoor Activities and Sports

Clarke Outdoors in West Cornwall (tel. 860/672–6365) offers canoe and kayak rentals as well as 10-mi trips from Falls Village to Housatonic Meadow State Park.

On Canaan Mountain, **Rustling Wind Stables** (tel. 860/824–7634) gives horseback-riding lessons and takes riders along scenic mountain trails.

Downhill skiers will find more than 40 mi and 23 trails (and man-made or natural snow) at **Mohawk Mountain** (tel. 860/672–6100) in Cornwall.

A special warm-weather local pastime is floating down the Farmington River on an inner tube rented (along with approved flotation devices) from **North American Canoe Tours** (tel. 860/739–0791) in New Hartford.

Restaurants

The face of northern Litchfield County's dining situation has changed considerably over the past couple years. Everyone still heads regularly to Canaan's old **Cannery Cafe** (85 Main St., tel. 860/824–7333), but its former menu of Cajun cooking and its dry-goods-store look have been replaced with a chic new American menu and crisp decor of off-white walls and brass wall fixtures. The formerly drab **Pub** (1 Station Pl., tel. 860/542–5716) in Norfolk has been reopened with an extremely diverse menu, half of it geared toward local deer hunters, the other half toward sophisticated antiques hunters—it's all good. Still popular are Winsted's **Tributary** (19 Rowley St., tel. 860/379–7679) for fresh seafood and scrumptious baked goods and Salisbury's **Chaiwalla** tea house (1 Main St., tel. 860/435–9758) for its scones, sandwiches, and more than 20 kinds of tea.

Nightlife and the Arts

The **Gilson Cafe and Cinema** (tel. 860/379–6069), a refurbished Art Deco movie house on Winsted's Main Street, serves food and drinks unobtrusively during movies, shown from Tuesday through Sunday evenings. You must be 21 or older to attend. Classical-music buffs head for not only the Norfolk Chamber Music Festival, but also for **Music Mountain** (Falls Village, 8 mi south of Canaan, off Rte. 7, tel. 860/824–7126) in summer.

Reservations Services

Bed & Breakfast, Ltd. (Box 216, New Haven 06513, tel. 203/469–3260), **Covered Bridge Bed & Breakfast Reservation Service** (Box 447, Norfolk 06058, tel. 860/542–5944), **Nutmeg Bed & Breakfast Agency** (Box 1117, West Hartford 06127, tel. 860/236–6698 or 800/727–7592).

Visitor Information

Litchfield Hills Travel Council (Box 968, Litchfield 06759, tel. 860/567–4506).

The Country Goose

Kent-Cornwall Rd. (Rte. 7), Kent 06757, tel. 860/927-4746

Three miles north of the only traffic light in Kent is a cozy, late-18th-century Colonial set on 5 acres near the Appalachian Trail. Owner Phyllis Dietrich, the daughter of a Viennese pastry chef, is usually in the kitchen whipping up scrumptious breakfast breads, muffins, and croissants . . . or the cookies she leaves out on the upstairs hall table for the couples and families with teens who temporarily call the Country Goose home. Sometimes you'll find her washing the immense windows that signify that the property's builder was well-to-do. Other relics of the building's earlier days are the beehive oven next to the Colonial fireplace in the breakfast room and detailed millwork throughout. Guest rooms are furnished with period reproductions and antiques, including such unusual pieces as a carved white-mahogany bed and a Victorian brass bed. Make yourself at home in the comfortable library or on the gazebo, where (if you ask nicely) Phyllis will serve you breakfast in the warmer months.

▦ *3 doubles and 1 single share 2 baths. Hiking (Appalachian Trail) nearby. $90; Continental breakfast. No credit cards. No smoking, no pets. 2-night minimum weekends. Closed Mar.–Apr. 10.*

Greenwoods Gate

105 Greenwoods Rd. E (Rte. 44), Norfolk 06058, tel. 860/542-5439, fax 860/542-5897

This neatly preserved Federal behind a 600-ft-long picket fence in secluded Norfolk seems unassuming enough. But what appears to be a quiet antiques shop, maybe, or a private home is in reality Connecticut's foremost romantic hideaway. Owner George Shumaker, formerly an executive with the Hilton hotel chain, is a cheerful host with a penchant for playing cupid.

He has spared nothing in providing all the trappings of a cozy honeymooners' retreat—he has probably even gone a little over the top. There are countless amenities in every room, from chocolates and Cognac to soaps, fresh flowers, and powders to board games with such titles as "Romantic Liaisons"; champagne or a deep massage are available with a little advance notice. The formal parlor, with its hardwood floors and authentic multipaned Federal windows, is decorated with period furnishings; it's a terrific place to meet other guests or chat with George. Most visitors, however, come here for one reason: romantic seclusion (best to leave the kids home). It's possible to stay here three days and without seeing another soul.

Of the four sumptuous suites, each with beds covered in starched white linens, the Levi Thompson Suite is the most interesting. Added later to the house, its entrance includes a short flight of stairs that leads to a small sitting area with a cathedral ceiling. Then, two more sets of stairs, both lined with solid cherry hand-tapered railings, lead to either side of an enormous master bed. If you haven't herniated a disk carrying your beloved over the threshold, plenty of fun awaits you in the suite's oversize spa bath. Recently, a spacious two-bedroom suite with its own den and library was added.

George likes to keep you well fed. He prepares a huge breakfast—a spread of muffins and fresh fruit followed by an extremely hearty hot meal—and offers a daily presentation of snacks, including afternoon wine and cheese.

Greenwoods Gate is a short drive from Tanglewood in the Berkshires and a stroll away from the site of the Norfolk Chamber Music Festival, but it's also miles from the headaches of urban living. Though the gruff and hard-hearted may find this setup a little too precious, couples who want to rekindle love's flame will be more than satisfied.

▦ *3 suites, 1 2-bedroom suite. Air-conditioning in rooms; whirlpool spa in*

1 suite; cable TV/VCR in common room. $175–$235; full breakfast. No credit cards. No smoking, no pets. 2-night minimum weekends.

Manor House

Box 447, Maple Ave., Norfolk 06058, tel. and fax 860/542–5690

A pleasant stroll up a side street off Norfolk's village green will bring you to a Bavarian Tudor residence that has been turned into a thriving B&B. After several years of working in Hartford's hectic insurance industry, owner-managers Diane and Henry Tremblay (who also own Covered Bridge Reservation Service) were both ready for a career change when they discovered an unusual house for sale. Designed and built in 1898 by Charles Spofford, the architect of London's subway system, the house has 20 stained-glass windows designed and given by Louis Tiffany, a full Victorian complement of reception rooms, and extensive bedrooms.

The Tremblays took over in 1985 and have gradually refurnished the inn and restored the Victorian atmosphere with a light touch. Henry devotes himself to the surrounding 5 acres of gardens, with beehives and a raspberry patch, whose yields find their way to the breakfast table.

The bedrooms are all furnished with antique and reproduction beds, Louis Nicole wallpapers, well-chosen bibelots, prints, ancestral photographs, mirrors, and carpets. In winter flannel sheets and down comforters add to the warmth. The vast Spofford Room has windows on three sides, a king-size canopy bed with a cheery fireplace opposite, and a balcony. The intimate Lincoln Room has an antique double sleigh bed, a white fainting couch, and a working fireplace— along with the best view of the neighboring landscape. But the Balcony Room has the most remarkable feature—a private, operational, wood-paneled elevator (added in 1939). It also has a private deck.

In the roomy living room, with its mammoth raised fireplace, music lovers who have come to Norfolk for the annual Chamber Music Festival (within easy walking distance) may choose from the large collection of compact discs. You may tickle the keys of the grand piano, or if you're in a quiet mood, seek the seclusion of the library and choose from its numerous volumes. (Note that this inn is not suitable for preteens).

▦ *7 doubles with bath, 1 2-bedroom suite. Working fireplaces in 3 rooms; Jacuzzi in 2 rooms; cable TV, house phone in common area. $115–$190; full breakfast. AE, MC, V. No smoking, no pets. 2-night minimum weekends; 3-night minimum holidays.*

Old Riverton Inn

Rte. 20, Riverton 06065, tel. 860/379–8678 or 800/378–1796, fax 860/379–1006

You can't miss the gray-blue and white Colonial frame building in Riverton: It's directly across from the Hitchcock Chair Factory, which is on the other side of the bridge that traverses the Farmington River. Tiny, serene Riverton was once called Hitchcockville, and the inn—a popular 18th-century stagecoach stop on the Hartford–Albany route—predates even the factory. Its present owners, Mark and Pauline Telford, continue the tradition of warm hospitality, particularly in the popular restaurant. It's open to the public for lunch and dinner Wednesday through Sunday and serves wholesome American favorites (chicken potpie, stuffed pork chops, and prime rib) amid a post-and-beam, Colonial-style decor.

Guest rooms here have the appealing architectural irregularity of age, but the decor—with its mixture of old and new—is less successful. The huge suite may have such amenities as wall-to-wall carpeting, a fireplace, and a minirefrigerator, but it distinctly lacks country-inn charm. The rooms on the third floor are generally smaller.

🏨 *11 doubles with bath, 1 suite. Restaurant; air-conditioning, cable TV in rooms; tubing, fishing, swimming nearby. $75–$110, suite $170; full breakfast. AE, D, DC, MC, V. Pets allowed with prior approval. 2-night minimum holiday weekends.*

Tollgate Hill Inn & Restaurant

Rte. 202 (Tollgate Hill Rd.), Litchfield 06759, tel. 860/567–4545 or 800/445–3903, fax 860/567–8397

On the north side of the road from Litchfield to Torrington, watch for the white sign that marks the entrance to the secluded Tollgate Inn. Since 1745 the main house (which was moved to its present site in 1923) has been a popular way station for travelers. The current proprietor, Fritz Zivic, is justifiably proud of the renovations that have been made to the place. Guest rooms are decorated with vibrant Colonial prints, checks, and stripes and have comfortable period-style furniture. The rooms and suites in the converted schoolhouse and Captain William Bull House that complete the complex have similar decor. Most have small sitting areas, including cozy tables for two next to multipaned windows that overlook the wooded grounds. All five suites and three of the rooms have fireplaces.

The tavern and the more formal dining room, celebrated for new American gourmet cuisine, hark back to the 18th century. Private parties take place in the ballroom—from its fiddlers' loft, musicians often serenade the diners below.

🏨 *15 doubles with bath, 5 suites. Restaurant; air-conditioning, cable TV, phones in rooms; bars, minirefrigerators, VCRs in suites. $110–$175; Continental breakfast. AE, D, DC. 2-night minimum holiday weekends.*

Under Mountain Inn

482 Undermountain Rd., Salisbury 06068, tel. 860/435–0242, fax 860/435–2379

Driving north on Route 41 from Salisbury's Main Street, you cut through sweeping fields where horses graze and silos rise in the distance. After about 4 mi, a stone's throw from the Massachusetts border, stands the Under Mountain Inn—a white clapboard farmhouse built in the early 1700s.

The owners, Marged and Peter Higginson, bill themselves as innkeepers and chefs, since the inn is also a popular restaurant. Their personal stamp—a part of which is defined by Peter's British origins—is found all over, from the decor of the intimate dining rooms (each with a working fireplace) to the VCR and extensive collection of British videos in Arabella's Lounge (named after Marged's grandmother and adorned with her prized antique china). In the back of the house is the pub, a faithful replica of a typical English taproom, whose paneling was found, during a restoration, beneath the attic floorboards. Since Colonial law awarded such choice lumber to the king of England, Peter reclaimed it in the name of the Crown.

Upstairs, the rooms are furnished in English country style. All have spectacular mountain views. Room names recall favorite London haunts: The spacious Downing Street has a queen-size bed; Buckingham Gate has one fit for a king; Drury Lane has a private entrance and a romantic canopy bed hung with mosquito netting. A decanter of sherry is found in each room, and Marged serves English tea and shortbread daily at 4 PM. With such pristine surroundings, parents traveling with young children should think twice about staying here.

Three surrounding acres boast birch, fir, maples, and a thorned locust tree, which is rumored to be the state's oldest. Across the road is Fisher Pond; you can use the 1.8-mi path around the pond for a bracing stroll—the form of exercise favored by the English.

For dinner, which along with a full breakfast is included in the cost, Peter prepares such specialties as steak-and-kidney pie, roast goose, or bangers and mash (sausage and mashed potatoes to the uninitiated). Save room for the English trifle—dessert par excellence.

🏨 *7 doubles with bath. Restaurant; air-conditioning in rooms. $170–$195; MAP, 7% service charge. MC, V. No smoking, no pets. 2-night minimum weekends.*

The White Hart

The Village Green, Box 385, Salisbury 06068, tel. 860/435–0030, fax 860/435–0040

With its fresh coat of white paint and its broad front porch, the White Hart really stands out on Salisbury's village green. This venerable country inn, which has welcomed travelers since the 1860s, fell on hard times in the 1980s. Before reopening in February 1990 owner-managers Terry and Juliet Moore renovated the place—inside and out. Their efforts show a respect for tradition and an appreciation of fine contemporary materials.

The green and rose carpeting in the lobby continues along the upstairs hallways, which also have champagne-striped wallpaper and white woodwork. Guest rooms and suites have excellent Colonial-reproduction furniture, good reading lamps, and modern bathrooms. Upholstery, bedspreads, and curtains are done in contrasting colors and patterns—a lively stripe here, a floral splash there, and maybe a colorful ribbon to tie it all together. Instead of tearing down walls to eliminate quirky room configurations, the quirks have been accommodated with pleasing results. Several rooms on the east side have private entrances, and a few steps away in the 1815 Gideon Smith House, similar rooms and suites are available on two levels.

In winter guests gather in the snug Hunt Room, with its wood paneling, roaring fireplace, and gleaming hardwood floors. In warmer weather the front porch, with its pink and white wicker love seats, colorful chintz, and trailing morning glory vines, is unbeatable. Dining in any of the White Hart's three restaurants—the bright and sunny Garden Room with its wall of French doors, the tavernlike Tap Room, or the elegant American Grill—is a pleasure.

🏨 *23 doubles with bath (1 is hall bath), 3 suites. 3 restaurants; air-conditioning, cable TV, phones in rooms; meeting rooms. $115–$195; breakfast extra. AE, DC, MC, V. Call about pets. 2-night minimum weekends Apr. 13–Nov. 15, 3-night minimum holiday weekends.*

Rhode Island

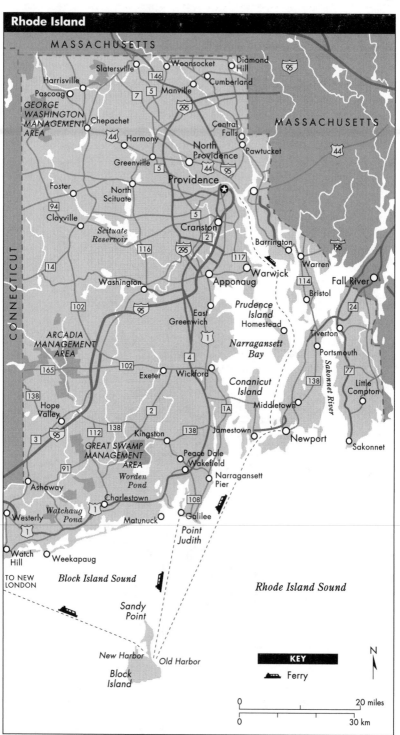

Rhode Island

MASSACHUSETTS

Slatersville • Woonsocket • Diamond Hill
146
Harrisville •
Pascoag •
7 • 5 • Manville • Cumberland
95

GEORGE WASHINGTON MANAGEMENT AREA
Chepachet •
295
Central Falls
MASSACHUSETTS
44
44 • Harmony •
North Providence
44
Pawtucket
Greenville • 5
95
Providence ★

Foster •
North Scituate
5

94
Clayville •
Scituate Reservoir
Cranston •
2
116 • 295
Barrington •
195
Warren •
117
Fall River •
24

14
Washington •
95
Apponaug •
Warwick •
114
Bristol •
Prudence Island
Homestead
Tiverton •
Portsmouth •

102
East Greenwich •
1
Narragansett Bay
138
77
Little Compton

ARCADIA MANAGEMENT AREA
4
Conanicut Island
Middletown •
Sakonnet River

165
102 • Exeter • Wickford •
1A
Jamestown •
Newport •
Sakonnet •

138
Hope Valley •
2
Kingston •
138
Peace Dale • Wakefield
Narragansett Pier
108

91
Ashaway •
Worden Pond
Charlestown •
1
Galilee •
Point Judith

Westerly •
Watchaug Pond
Matunuck •

1
Watch Hill • Weekapaug •
Block Island Sound

TO NEW LONDON
Sandy Point

Rhode Island Sound

New Harbor / Old Harbor

Block Island

KEY

N

Ferry

0 — 20 miles
0 — 30 km

Newport

The Inn at Castle Hill

Perched gloriously at the mouth of the Narragansett Bay, world-famous Newport has four substantial claims: It's one of the great sailing cities of the world, for many years the site of the annual America's Cup yacht race; it boasts a peerless collection of late-19th-century mansions; there are over 200 pre-Revolutionary buildings here, more than in any other city in the country; and it hosts world-class jazz, folk, and classical music festivals every summer.

Newport's first age of prosperity, the Golden Age, was in the mid-1700s, when some of the New World's best artisans and businessmen resided here. Many homes, churches, and government buildings from the Colonial era still stand. Most of these are now restored, and many are open to visitors. Unfortunately, Newport's wondrous Colonial past is often overlooked, its appeal eclipsed by the city's grandiose Gilded Age mansions and its posh social fabric.

During the mid- to late 19th century, Newport became the fashionable summer playground of America's wealthiest families. Having taken the grand tour of Europe and seen its magnificent castles, the well-to-do displayed their newfound *sophistication by building their own extravagant mansion-size "cottages" along Newport's Bellevue Avenue. Each cottage was more elaborate than the one built just before it, culminating in the grandiose excess of Cornelius Vanderbilt II's The Breakers, which today would cost approximately $400 million to duplicate.*

Newport on a summer afternoon can be exasperating, its streets jammed with day-trippers, its traffic slowed to a crawl by a succession of air-conditioned sightseeing buses. Yet it's worth braving the crowds to attend the city's summer music festivals—the Newport Music Festival for 10 days in mid-July (tel. 401/846–1133), the Rhythm & Blues Festival July 25–27, and the Ben & Jerry's Folk Festival and JVC Jazz Festival— both in August (tel. 401/847–3700 for the three events). In the fall, winter, and spring, you can enjoy a visit to Newport without having to contend with crowds, although from mid-November to March, many of the mansions are open only on weekends. The weather stays fairly warm well into November, and there are many special events in December as the city celebrates "Christmas in Newport."

Places to Go, Sights to See

The Breakers (Ochre Point Ave., tel. 401/847–6543). Beginning in 1893, it took 2,500 workers two years to complete this 70-room summer home for the small family of Cornelius Vanderbilt II; 40 servants were required to keep the establishment running. The four-story limestone villa is loaded with marvels: There's a music room with a gold ceiling, a fireplace built of rare blue marble, rose alabaster pillars in the dining room, and a porch with a mosaic ceiling that took Italian craftsmen six months lying on their backs to install.

Cliff Walk. This 3-mi-long trail, which begins at Easton's Beach and runs along Newport's eastern edge, offers a waterside view of many of the city's mansions. (Note that although this path is generally smooth, sections of it are unpaved and rocky; the walk is best suited to those who are sure of foot.)

Hammersmith Farm (Ocean Dr. near Ft. Adams, tel. 401/846–7346). The childhood summer home of Jacqueline Bouvier Kennedy Onassis, this estate overlooking the Narragansett Bay brings meaning to the term Kennedy Camelot. The graceful, magical house is decorated in such a casual, comfortable style and is filled with so much Bouvier and Kennedy memorabilia that it feels as if its owners temporarily stepped out of the room. The elaborate grounds were designed by Frederick Law Olmsted, known for his work on New York City's Central Park.

International Tennis Hall of Fame and the **Tennis Museum** (Newport Casino, 194 Bellevue Ave., tel. 401/849–3990). This component of the Newport Casino building, which was designed by Stanford White, features new multimedia exhibits, photographs, and other artifacts celebrating a century of tennis history. The first National Tennis Championships were held here in 1881.

Museum of Yachting (Ft. Adams and Ocean Dr., tel. 401/847–1018). Set at the water's edge is beautiful Ft. Adams State Park. This showcase of boating history allows you to browse galleries with pictures of the incredible yachts of the Vanderbilts, the Astors, and the Belmonts.

Brick Market (Thames St., tel. 401/841–8770). Slaves were bought and sold in this Federal-style market building known as the Brick Market. It now houses the superb *Museum of Newport History*. Impressive multimedia exhibits explore Newport's social and economic influences, while antiques, such as James Franklin's printing press, inspire the imagination.

Redwood Library (50 Bellevue Ave., tel. 401/847–0292). Built in 1748, this library is a superb example of the work of noted Colonial architect Peter Harrison. The wooden building, designed to look like a Roman temple, has its exterior painted to resemble marble. Inside you'll find a wonderful collection of paintings by Early American artists.

Trinity Church (Queen Anne Sq., tel. 401/846–0660). Built in 1724, this Colonial treasure is especially notable for its three-tier wineglass pulpit, the only one of its kind in America.

Beaches

Easton's Beach (Memorial Blvd.), known locally as First Beach, is popular for its carousel. **Sachuest Beach** (Sachuest Point area), also called Second Beach, is adjacent to the Norman Bird Sanctuary; dunes, a sometimes-heavy surf, and a campground make it popular among singles and surfers. **Third Beach** (Sachuest Point area), on the Sakonnet River, has a boat ramp and is a favorite of wind-surfers.

Restaurants

At the **Black Pearl** (Bannister's Wharf, tel. 401/846–5264), a popular waterfront restaurant with nautical decor, you can choose between the tavern and the more formal Commodore's Room (jacket required). Recommended is swordfish with Dutch pepper butter. **La Forge Casino Restaurant** (186 Bellevue Ave., tel. 401/847–0418) is inside the gracious, shingle-style Casino building designed by McKim, Mead, and White for Newport's Gilded Age elite. The food is average, but the genteel atmosphere and the view of the Casino's perfect grass tennis courts are pure Newport. **The Place** (28 Washington Sq., tel. 401/847–0125) is a local favorite. A wide-ranging menu with all-original dishes is this establishment's forte. The adjoining bar has 36 beers on tap.

Reservations Services

Anna's Victorian Connection (5 Fowler Ave., Newport 02840, tel. 401/849–2489 or 800/884–4288), **Bed and Breakfast Newport** (33 Russell Ave., Newport 02840, tel. 401/846–5408), **Bed and Breakfast of Rhode Island, Inc.** (Box 3291, Newport 02840, tel. 401/849–1298).

Visitor Information

Newport County Convention and Visitors Bureau (23 America's Cup Ave., Newport 02809, tel. 401/849–8048 or 800/326–6030) has telephones linked to motels for placing reservations, an orientation film, and cassette tours.

Admiral Fitzroy Inn

398 Thames St., 02840, tel. 401/848–8000 or 800/343–2863, fax 401/848–8006

To make way for a parking lot, the Admiral Fitzroy—once a convent adjacent to St. Mary's Church, where Jacqueline Bouvier and John F. Kennedy were married—was moved down the hill to Thames Street nine years ago. The 1854 structure has since been fancifully redecorated. Owner Jane Berriman and an artistic friend hand-painted the walls, the trim, and much of the furniture. One room sports shiny green walls and ceiling trim of interlocking leaves and scallop shells; another features a blue sponge-painted surface with a cheerful border of wildflowers. There are sleigh beds and brass bedsteads (mostly reproduction Victorian pieces) all covered with down duvets and lacy linens. In each room a handmade Swedish cupboard contains a TV, a refrigerator, and an electric tea kettle. Two of the rooms have private decks.

The spacious lobby has an atmosphere as cheery as the rooms. A rooftop deck with a superb view of Newport Harbor was added in 1995. The clean, bright Admiral Fitzroy may not be a good choice if you prefer quiet evenings; because of its proximity to the marinas, the inn is popular with sailors—a historically festive lot.

🏨 *18 doubles with bath. Air-conditioning, phones, TVs, refrigerators, tea pots, hair dryers in rooms; elevator; free parking. $125–$195; full breakfast, afternoon tea. AE, DC, MC, V. 2-night minimum summer weekends, 3-night minimum holiday weekends and festivals.*

Cliffside Inn

2 Seaview Ave., 02840, tel. 401/847–1811 or 800/845–1811, fax 401/848–5850

This spellbinding Victorian B&B sits on a shady side street just up from Newport's Cliff Walk. The Cliffside Inn's charm does not necessarily stem from its remarkable amenities, refinements, and accolades; nor is it based in the well-mannered, expert services of innkeeper Stan Nicholas. Rather, the remarkable appeal of this inn radiates from the life story of a recluse whose paintings now adorn walls in all 15 rooms.

Maryland governor Thomas Swann built the home in 1880 as a retreat from his war-beleaguered state. In 1891 the home was sold to a Philadelphia cotton merchant whose 17-year-old daughter, Beatrice, was the love of his life. The fawning father had her removed from art school upon learning of her work with nude models. "Paint me a picture of yourself," he reportedly said.

After she died of malnutrition in 1948, townspeople discovered that Beatrice Turner—who lived for 35 years in a mansion painted black, had no friends, and dressed herself each day in Victorian clothing—had rendered 1,000 self-portraits in oil. Only 150 of her paintings survive. But thanks to the upgrades made by current owner Win Baker, the inn now has a sterling image, a polished repose that turns the eerie mystique of Beatrice Turner into outright charm.

Filled with cozy nooks and crannies and flooded with sunlight from its many bay windows and skylights, the Cliffside is a titillating place. Just off the large center hallway, with its original gleaming hardwood floor and double doors, is a spacious parlor that has a Victorian fireplace bedecked with an ornate antique mirror. (Note that this inn's wealth of knickknacks and antiques makes it inappropriate for children.)

The guest rooms are decorated with Victorian furniture and Laura Ashley fabrics, and each room has a name that recalls past residents or refers to its decor. The Governor's Suite—the inn's most luxurious quarters—has a king-size four-poster bed, a whirlpool bath, an antique birdcage shower, and an unusual two-sided fireplace (one side is in the bedroom, the other in the bathroom). Some rooms have fireplaces, and others have whirlpool baths (a few have both).

🏨 *8 doubles with bath, 7 suites. Air-conditioning, cable TV, phones in rooms. $145–$305; full breakfast, afternoon tea. AE, D, DC, MC, V. No smoking, no pets.*

Elm Tree Cottage

336 Gibbs Ave., 02840, tel. 401/849–1610 or 800/882–3356, fax 401/849–2084

In a quiet, tree-shaded neighborhood between Easton's Pond and Bellevue Avenue is the incomparable Elm Tree Cottage. The elegantly designed shingle-style house was built in 1882 by architect William Ralph Emerson (Ralph Waldo's cousin), who is best known for his stick-style Maine homes. Owners Priscilla and Thomas Malone—look for their stained-glass work throughout the home—bought the Elm Tree in 1989, when the city granted them special exception to run a B&B in a residential zone, a good-faith effort designed to save this architectural treasure from condominium plans.

Each massive room (often with a fireplace), furnished with French and English antiques and decorated by Priscilla, is an interior-design vignette. The Windsor Suite is more than 1,000 square ft and is fitted with a fireplace, a stereo, and a king-size bed with carved Louis XV headboard and canopy.

The spacious living room has two pianos and overlooks ½-acre of gardens. You can help yourself to soft drinks or mix BYOB cocktails at the bar, which resembles the cabin of a yacht. (Although older children may enjoy the lawn and the common rooms, this inn is too upscale for little ones.)

Priscilla is also known for her creative, gourmet breakfasts. Homemade French-toast soufflé topped with whipped maple cream or a Florentine phyllo cup with a béarnaise sauce are served on white-linen tables and accompanied by a poem or a thought for the day.

🏨 *6 doubles with bath. Air-conditioning. $175–$325; full breakfast. AE, MC, V. No smoking, no pets. 2-night minimum weekends, 3-night minimum holiday weekends. Closed Dec. 24–26.*

Francis Malbone House

392 Thames St., 02840, tel. 401/846–0392, fax 401/848–5956

This brick Colonial mansion on bustling Thames Street was built in 1760 by Colonel Francis Malbone, a shipping magnate who, to avoid paying English taxes, ran a tunnel from the cellar to the pier where his ships landed. Ironically, the British used the adjacent "counting house"—which is now one of Newport's finest guest suites—as a gold storehouse during the Revolutionary War.

The home is listed on the National Register of Historic Places and is believed to have been designed by Peter Harrison (the architect responsible for the nearby Touro Synagogue and Redwood Library). The structure was immaculately restored from 1968 to 1974, and is now Newport's only Colonial mansion operating as an inn. It's only a 10-minute walk from Washington Square, a plus for visitors interested in historic Newport. However, the noise from tourist-thick Thames Street may induce light sleepers to opt for a room at the back.

In 1996, at a cost of $1 million, a 10-room addition was built; at the same time, a formal dining room with a domed ceiling, recessed lighting, and dental molding was added. All the new rooms have four-poster king-size beds, Jacuzzi baths, and fireplaces. The colonnade, which opens onto a courtyard and extends to the new wing, has 12 beautiful blue-on-white Portuguese baroque tiles. These "greeting figure" tiles were a popularly traded commodity during the time the Frances Malbone House was built.

All three public rooms are tastefully furnished with Colonial reproduction pieces and antiques. The original kitchen has an authentic Colonial brick fireplace with a beehive oven; tea and snacks are served here every afternoon. The full gourmet breakfast includes a main dish made-to-order; cereal and pastries are available at a buffet table.

Young innkeepers Mary Frances Mahaffey, Stephanie Walmsey, and Will Dewey are warm and welcoming. Repeat guests rave about the highly professional service and the elegant, gracious atmosphere (one that young children may not appreciate).

🏨 *18 doubles with bath. Whirlpool baths in 10 rooms, fireplaces in 15 rooms, free parking. $165–$325; full breakfast. AE, MC, V. No smoking.*

The Inn at Castle Hill

Ocean Dr., 02840, tel. 401/849–3800

The Inn at Castle Hill is perched in jaunty isolation on a 40-acre peninsula with its own private beach. Built as a summer home for scientist and explorer Alexander Agassiz, the inn is a rambling shingled structure, with curves, gingerbread woodwork, turrets, and jutting porches imitating the chalets of Dr. Agassiz's native Switzerland. Outbuildings dot the grounds, including Agassiz's former laboratory (which may be rented as a suite), a series of beach cottages (rented by the week), and the six Harbor Houses, where Grace Kelly lived while filming *High Society*.

Inside, many original furnishings reflect Agassiz's fondness for Chinese and Japanese art, particularly bronzes and porcelain (owing to all the fine pieces, it's best to leave children at home). The lounge, with Asian rugs and richly patterned period wallpaper, has two small Victorian sofas nestled next to an unusual hand-carved fireplace—its design reminiscent of a stained-glass rose window in a Gothic cathedral. Three water-view dining rooms include the professor's original study, the Sunset Room, and the original dining room. The superb restaurant is particularly popular for Sunday brunch; on summer Sunday afternoons the Inn holds a barbecue with music that has become de rigueur.

The seven spacious oceanside rooms in the main house, which must be booked months in advance, are furnished with Victorian antiques and comfortable chairs, decorated with bright floral fabrics, and have enormous bathrooms. Room 6, with a large bay window, was built for Mrs. Agassiz; Room 7, Dr. Agassiz's bedroom, has walls and a ceiling of inlaid oak and pine; Room 8, decorated with white wicker furniture, features an old claw-foot tub and a view of the bay and the Newport Bridge; Room 9, pentagonal in shape, was mentioned in *Theophilus North*, a Thorton Wilder novel based in Newport. An upstairs suite combines a large living room and a bedroom. The six-unit Harbor House was recently renovated; each unit has a king-size bed, a Jacuzzi, and a private deck. For many repeat guests, the inn's antique and somewhat creaky charms, along with its fabulous views and private beach, convey the true essence of Newport.

🏨 *21 doubles with bath, 3 doubles share 1 bath, 1 suite, 18 seasonal doubles with bath. Restaurant (closed weekdays Nov.–mid Apr.), private beach. $135–$325; Continental breakfast. AE, MC, V. No pets. 2-night minimum summer weekends.*

The Inntowne

6 Mary St., 02840, tel. 401/846–9200 or 800/457–7803, fax 401/846–1534

Behind the Dutch door of this large gray, clapboard building just off bustling Thames Street is a stately pinewood lobby and a welcoming, professional staff. The big, clean guest rooms are decorated with floral wallpaper and Colonial reproduction pieces that create an ambience somewhere between "rustic tavern" and "motel modern." Light sleepers should ask for a room on one of the upper floors, a ways up from the traffic noise.

The fourth floor Wicker Room has a view of the harbor. Eight deluxe rooms have love seats and a desk. A fourth-floor sun-deck with tables, umbrellas, and lounge chairs is an excellent place to unwind before or after dinner.

🏨 *26 doubles with bath. Phones in rooms, kitchen facilities in some rooms, small patios off some rooms, 24-hr concierge, access to nearby health club. $139–$179; Continental breakfast. AE, MC, V. No no-smoking rooms available.*

Ivy Lodge

12 Clay St., 02840, tel. 401/849–6865

Just inside this elegant Queen Anne Victorian, designed by Stanford White, is an amazing sight: a 33-ft-high Gothic-style oak-paneled entry with a three-story staircase and a dangling wrought-iron chandelier. Just off the foot of the staircase is a brick fireplace built in the shape of a Moorish arch. A welcoming fire burns here on chilly afternoons.

Ivy Lodge, which was built in 1886 for a prominent New York physician, has eight spacious guest rooms—all taste-fully decorated with a combination of Victorian antiques and good-quality reproductions. Newporters and veteran innkeepers Maggie and Terry Moy live at Ivy Lodge. Their manner is low-key and gracious, their rates are reasonable, and they know how to make you very comfortable.

The Turret Room, decorated in peach and green, has a king-size bed and a pri-vate bath with a Victorian claw-foot tub. The Ivy Room has a queen-size four-poster bed with French-cut white linens, Waverly ivy wallpaper, and a private bath. A set of Herend dishes for the din-ing room has an ivy pattern.

The sumptuous breakfast served here might include such delicacies as smoked fish, homemade quiche, bread pudding, or fresh strawberries and popovers with whipped cream. A 20-ft-long mahogany table that seats 18 dominates the long dining room, with floor-to-ceiling bay windows at one end. The bright main floor sitting room has floral wallpaper and wicker furniture; it's also invitingly full of books and magazines. The airy living room features pink-and-white-striped Art Deco sofas, thick carpeting, and a huge fireplace. The wraparound front porch with cushioned wicker chairs is popular with summer guests.

Although Ivy Lodge is neither as large nor as opulent as the fabled mansions on nearby Bellevue Avenue, it is every bit as gracious.

🏨 *8 doubles with bath. $100–$180; full breakfast. AE, MC, V. No smoking.*

Sanford-Covell Villa Marina

72 Washington St., 02840, tel. 401/847–0206

This elegant Eastlake-style home, with its spindlework detailing, was built in 1869 as a summer residence for Milton H. Sanford by architect William Ralph Emerson. In 1895 the house was sold to William Covell, and it is still owned by two of his descendants, Anne and Richard Cuvelier.

Inside the house elaborately carved wooden balconies open onto an entrance hall that soars 35 ft. The authenticity of this Gilded Age home is startling; in fact, from 1972 to 1980, the home was a mu-seum run by the Society for the Protec-tion of New England Antiquities. When the Culveliers reassumed the deed, a clause stipulated that nothing could be changed; so it is that a public coffeemaker sits on a table dating from the 1700s.

A few of the amazing features include black walnut wainscoted walls, parquet floors in each room, original glass globes on bronze chandeliers, and walls deco-rated with original frescoes. Just beyond a gorgeous, heated, black-bottom pool, a private dock juts into Newport Harbor.

⊞ *6 doubles, 3 with shared bath. Heated saltwater pool. $65–$225; Continental breakfast, afternoon refreshments. No credit cards. 2-night minimum in summer.*

Victorian Ladies

63 Memorial Blvd., 02840, tel. 401/849–9960

The location of the Victorian Ladies on busy Memorial Boulevard may, at first, give pause. But once you're inside, double-pane windows and air-conditioning muffle the street noise. In addition, the sumptuous furnishings and the friendly attention of hosts Don and Helene O'Neill fully compensate for any din that might slip through.

Don and Helene bought their home in 1985 after a B&B trip to California convinced them that they would enjoy being hosts at their own establishment. They purchased a fairly rundown home and carriage house built around 1840. The former occupants were elderly women who seemed to have stepped straight out of the Victorian era—thus the name. Thanks to his years of experience in restoration carpentry, Don was able to renovate the place himself.

The mansard exterior of the Victorian Ladies is now painted deep green and burgundy. Nine dormer windows are accented by scalloped wood shingles and curvaceous moldings. The main house and the carriage house are connected by a flower-filled latticed courtyard that serves as an outdoor breakfast area in the summer. Recent additions include a formal garden with vine-covered brick walls.

The living room, mauve and light blue, has a crystal chandelier, a cozy fireplace, floral wallpaper, several plump-pillowed couches, and many ornamental objects from the Far East. The adjoining dining room has more of a country feeling, with a Welsh dresser and a large English-pine table and sideboard, where ample traditional breakfasts of eggs and bacon or ham are served.

The rooms are furnished with an eclectic collection of antiques, reproductions, and modern pieces, that, through Helene's visual tastes, harmoniously coexist. Each room has a canopy, sleigh, or four-poster bed and colorful wallpaper. A favorite of many guests is the Honeymoon Suite. As in so many other rooms in the inn, the bed here is heaped with ruffled pillows handmade by Helene. Another guest room features children's lace dresses on the walls, set off by a black background with a rosebud print. A third has birdcage wallpaper, birdcages painted on cabinetry, and, of course, a Victorian-era birdcage. (Such details make this an inappropriate place for children.)

⊞ *11 doubles with bath. Air-conditioning, TVs in rooms; free parking. $135–$185; full breakfast. MC, V. No smoking.*

Coastal Rhode Island

The Richards

When the old Route 1 was superseded by the northerly routed
I–95 in the 1960s, something wonderful happened—or rather
didn't happen. Coastal Rhode Island (South County, as it's
known locally, though the real name is Washington County)
was left behind in time. The 19th-century resorts of Watch Hill
and Narragansett, with their immense summer homes,
maintained an air of genteel refuge. The quiet town of Westerly,
just over the border from Connecticut, has a remarkable
number of fine old homes as well as summer residents who,
like their parents and grandparents before them, think the
world of their piece of the New England coast. Kingston, which
contains the shady green campus of the University of Rhode
Island, has kept all the charm of a college town without
surrendering to tacky development. In fact the region as a
whole is surprisingly unblighted by the march of malls and
tract housing that has overtaken other, more accessible areas.

Much of the rolling landscape of slow-paced South County is
still farmland—in fact, north of Narragansett, in Rhode
Island's so-called plantation country, many farms dating
from the Colonial era are intact; some of them can be visited
today. With 19 preserves, state parks, beaches, and forest

areas, including three in Charlestown alone—Burlingame State Park, Ninigret Park, and the Trustom Pond Wildlife Refuge—South County is a region that respects the concept of wilderness. But for summertime visitors, the area's most important attraction is its 25-mi strip of broad, sandy beaches.

Places to Go, Sights to See

Galilee. This village sits at the south end of the Narragansett peninsula, off Route 108. As you might expect from Rhode Island's busiest fishing port, Galilee has two excellent seafood restaurants: *Champlin's* (tel. 401/783–3152) and *George's of Galilee* (tel. 401/783–2306). Galilee is the point of departure for several excursion boats and a ferry (tel. 401/783–4613) to Block Island.

Narragansett Pier. At the end of the 19th century, many wealthy vacationers from New York and Boston arrived by train at this posh resort; others took the steamboat over from Newport to visit the Narragansett Casino. Though the railroad and steamboat no longer operate, a section of the casino survived a disastrous 1900 fire: *The Towers* has impressive and unusual Victorian turrets that rise above Ocean Road; it now houses the Narragansett Chamber of Commerce. At the end of Ocean Road, there's a beautiful vista at the *Point Judith Lighthouse.*

South County Museum (Canochet Farm Rd., tel. 401/783–5400). On the grounds of Canonchet Farm, this unusual museum has seven buildings housing 20,000 artifacts dating from 1800 to 1933. Exhibits include a country kitchen, a carpentry shop, a working print shop, an antique carriage collection, and more.

Watch Hill. This Victorian beach village (actually a part of Westerly) is a good place to shop for jewelry, summer clothes, and antiques. Stop by to watch hand-carved ponies whirl on the *Flying Horses Carousel,* the oldest merry-go-round in America (built in 1867), then stroll out on Napatree Point, a long sandy spit with a protected wildlife area.

Westerly. Westerly was once distinguished for its flawless blue granite, from which monuments throughout the country were made. The town's 18-acre *Wilcox Park,* at the intersection of High and Broad streets, was designed by Frederick Law Olmsted and Calvert Vaux and has a garden for people with vision impairments (names of flowers are posted in braille) and other disabilities. Nearby is the 1736 Babcock-Smith House (124 Granite St., tel. 401/596–5704), where Benjamin Franklin was a frequent visitor.

Beaches

Busy **Misquamicut State Beach** (Rte. 1A, Westerly) is popular with young and old for its beachside rides and games, yet many locals decry its tackiness. **East**

Beach (Off Rte. 1, access from East Beach Rd., Charlestown) offers 2 mi of dunes, backed by the clear waters of Ninigret Pond. **East Matunuck State Beach** (South of Rte. 1, off Succotash Rd., Mantunuck) features high surf, picnic areas, and a bathhouse.

Restaurants

In addition to places listed *under* Galilee *above,* try **Shelter Harbor Inn** (10 Wagner Rd., Westerly, tel. 401/322–8883), which offers gourmet Continental dining in a tranquil country setting. **Chez Pascal** (944 Boston Neck Rd., South Kingstown, tel. 401/782–6020) serves French cuisine in an intimate setting; make reservations early on weekends. **Aunt Carrie's** (Rte. 108 and Ocean Rd., Point Judith, tel. 401/783–7930) has traditional Rhode Island shore dinners (steamed clams, lobster, corn on the cob, coleslaw, and clam chowder) on summer evenings.

Nightlife

The **Ocean Mist** (Matunuck, tel. 401/782–3740) is a classic roadhouse bar on the dunes along Matunuck Beach Road; you'll find live music here most nights of the week. The **Coast Guard House** (tel. 401/789–0700), right on the seawall in Narragansett, has a bar that's popular for after-dinner drinks.

Reservations Service

Bed and Breakfast of Rhode Island, Inc. (Box 3291, Newport 02840, tel. 401/ 849–1298).

Visitor Information

South County Tourism Council (Box 651, Narragansett 02882, tel. 401/789– 4422 or 800/548–4662).

Admiral Dewey Inn

668 Matunuck Beach Rd., South Kingstown 02879, tel. 401/783-2090

Built in 1898 as a summer boardinghouse for blue-collar Rhode Islanders, this shingled, three-story inn stood unused for many years until Joan Lebel, a former teacher, bought it and restored it to its original condition in 1989.

The inn is listed on the National Register of Historic Places, and its 10 guest rooms—some have ocean views, others are cozy and tucked in the eaves—have been furnished with matching sets of ornately carved Victorian-style cabinets and hutches.

A Continental breakfast is set out at an 1840 harvest table that expands to seat 40. Beachgoing and summer-stock theater (the top-notch Theatre By-The-Sea is within walking distance) are the prime summertime activities. You'll also find live music just down the street at the Ocean Mist beach bar. The Admiral Dewey is a great base from which to explore all of what Joan calls the "always-casual southern shore" (ask about convenient day trips to Block Island).

⊞ *8 doubles with bath, 2 doubles share bath. $80–$125; Continental breakfast. MC, V. No smoking.*

Ocean House

2 Bluff Ave., Watch Hill 02891, tel. 401/348-8161

The immensity of the Ocean House, a yellow-clapboard Victorian hotel, will take your breath away. Built by George Nash in 1868, this was one of the grand hotels that helped earn Watch Hill its fame as a 19th-century resort. Although it looks a bit unkempt, this enormous summer retreat has one of the best seaside porches in New England.

In operation since just after the Civil War, the inn has been run by the Brankert family since 1938 (Grandpa Brankert bought it just before the 1938 hurricane, explains his grandson Michael, the current assistant manager). You'll enjoy magnificent sunset views from the immense porch. The restaurant, housed in a cheerful setting of ballroom proportions, serves three hearty meals a day (two are included in the room price). A set of rickety stairs leads down to a spectacular private ocean beach.

Room furnishings are not distinguished—basic maple chests, bedside tables, and desks and chairs—but almost every room has an ocean view (corner rooms have the best). Such panoramas make creaky beds and unpolished floors seem trivial.

⊞ *56 doubles with bath, 3 singles with bath. Restaurant, lounge. $185–$210; breakfast, dinner. MC, V. No pets. 2-night minimum weekends, 3-night minimum holidays. Closed Labor Day–late June.*

The Richards

144 Gibson Ave., Narragansett 02882, tel. 401/789-7746

This English manor–style home, built of granite quarried nearby, is a most unusual B&B. Joseph Peace Hazard, scion of a locally prominent industrialist family, reportedly built this fortresslike home in 1884 because of the property's excellent well water. He never lived in the house, and what exactly this transcendentalist baron and his guests did here is something of a mystery. Hazard had the words DRUID'S DREAM carved over the doorway. The owners of 11 years, Nancy and Steven Richards, will be happy to share what they know about the inn's intriguing history and the doorway's peculiar reference.

Meticulously restored and listed on the National Register of Historic Places, the Richards has a broodingly Gothic mystique that is almost the antithesis of a summer home. But the rooms are very comfortable, and the neighborhood is quiet (though construction crews have recently been putting up homes nearby). Each guest room is furnished with 19th-century English antiques and has a working fireplace, down comforters, and floral-upholstered or wicker couches and chairs. Nancy serves a breakfast of fresh fruit, strudel, cereal, coffee, and muffins, as well as such main courses as eggs Florentine and oven pancakes.

French windows look out onto a lush landscape, with a grand swamp oak the centerpiece of a handsome garden. On chilly afternoons you'll find the library fireplace ablaze. You can walk a nature trail to the rocky coast and then to sandy Narragansett Beach. Fine restaurants are also within walking distance.

Many guests spend an entire week, as Newport and Block Island are easy to reach from here. Though Nancy and Steven are welcoming, this is not a B&B for travelers who desire a great deal of personal attention; Nancy is quick to point out that this is a family home first, and a business second.

▥ *2 doubles with bath, 2 doubles share bath, 1 2-bedroom suite. $60–$160; full breakfast. No credit cards. No smoking, no pets. 2-night minimum summer weekends, 3-night minimum holidays.*

Shelter Harbor Inn

10 Wagner Rd., Westerly 02891, tel. 401/ 322–8883

This inn and large restaurant is an institution in South County. During the past 70 years, the 1810 farmhouse has been a commune, a country club with stables, a nursing home, and an inn. In 1912 the 200-acre oceanside property became an off-season music colony for Newport summer performers. Over a dozen streets surrounding the inn are still named for famous musicians.

When current owner Jim Dye took over the property 20 years ago, the inn had essentially declined to a boardinghouse. "Kicking the boarders out was the best

thing I could do. They all ended up buying houses!" says owner Jim Dye, a self-described Wall Street exile who spent childhood summers in Westerly.

The lobby, library, and sunporch are decorated with such quirky antiques as an enormous Hoosier hutch and a Simplex wall clock. The guest rooms are furnished with a combination of Victorian antiques and reproduction pieces; bedspreads and curtains are in muted floral patterns.

Most of the rooms have working fireplaces; some have decks (the corner room, Number 9, is a particular favorite). It should be noted that on damp spring days the pervasive musty scent of ashes can make fireplaces disagreeable.

The surrounding 4 acres include a croquet lawn, paddle-tennis courts, two patios, and a swing set (children are welcome at the inn). Men's and women's locker rooms open onto a rooftop replete with a barbecue grill and a massive stainless-steel hot tub. A shuttle bus runs on the hour to the private beach, one of the best stretches of sand in the state. (If you want to go to the beach on check-out day, you're welcome to use the locker rooms.)

Breakfast is right off the restaurant's menu, which typically includes banana-walnut French toast, eggs Benedict, and smoked haddock served over johnny-cakes (an Ocean State favorite).

A few older guests fondly recall the property as an equestrian camp. Essentially, that healthful, cheery summer-camp atmosphere perseveres.

▥ *23 doubles with bath. Restaurant; bar; air-conditioning, TVs, phones in rooms; paddle tennis; croquet. $92–$126; full breakfast. AE, D, MC, V. No pets. 2-night minimum weekends Memorial Day–Thanksgiving, 3-night minimum holidays.*

Stone Lea

40 Newton Ave., Narragansett 02882, tel. 401/783-9546, fax 401/792-8237

Off Ocean Drive in a section called Millionaire's Mile is Stone Lea, a dignified shingle-covered house with lines of sight across Narragansett Bay to Newport, Jamestown, Tiverton, and Block Island. Situated a mile south of Narragansett, this classic house (circa 1884) was designed by the famous architectural firm of McKim, Mead, and White, which was also responsible for the Rhode Island Statehouse and Narragansett's most recognized buildings: the Coast Guard House, the Towers, and the Casino. Built primarily of Rhode Island granite, this B&B is as solid as it is beautiful.

Rotundas and bay windows protrude hither and yon. Inside you'll find big windows, lots of light, and such elaborate details as carved wood paneling in the main entrance hall, a grand-piano staircase that rises from the parquet floor of the large foyer, and a Dutch door with inch-thick beveled glass. Off the entryway is an ostentatiously large living room; bright and inviting, it has a sunporch.

Stone Lea functioned as a B&B for eight years prior to its 1995 purchase by current live-in owner and surgeon Guy Lancellotti, who is fond of putting the business's income back into the house. Recent upgrades include new mattresses and linens for all the rooms, restoration of all the wooden floors and wainscoting, and new Asian rugs. Vivacious innkeeper Sara Incollingo serves a full breakfast in the well-appointed dining room.

A few guest rooms (the Block Island Room is one) have unbeatable views, but all have at least a glimpse of the water. The four larger rooms offer truly top-notch accommodations that are worth the extra money. Despite the amazing architecture, Stone Lea's most memorable feature is its broad lawn, at the end of which a shoulder of flat rock runs along the shore of Narragansett Bay. Guests can hike along this field of stone all the way to Scarboro Beach, a favorite of Rhode Island's sunbathers. Stone Lea is also within walking distance of restaurants and shops in the shore village of Narragansett Pier.

🏠 *7 doubles with bath. Cable TV in common area. $100–$150; full breakfast. AE, MC, V. No smoking, no pets. 2-day minimum summer weekends, 3-night minimum holidays. Closed Thanksgiving and Dec. 25.*

Weekapaug Inn

25 Spring Ave., Weekapaug 02891, tel. 401/322-0301

At the end of curving Ninigret Avenue—past a line of gracious, vintage, beachfront homes—waits an enchanting inn where time seems to have stopped circa 1939. The Weekapaug Inn has been operated in summer by members of the Buffum family since 1899—with only one interruption: the hurricane of 1938. Even in the face of that catastrophe, the family acted quickly, rebuilding the destroyed inn from scratch several hundred yards from its former waterside site and reopening just one week late in the summer of 1939.

The building seems more a mansion than an inn, with a peaked roof, a stone foundation, and a huge wraparound porch. It was rebuilt to withstand a major hurricane (it has a steel understructure) and is on a peninsula in salty Quonochontaug Pond. There's a comfy tidiness about the furnishings throughout; the guest-room decor is cheerful though not particularly remarkable. Each room is big and has large windows with impressive views.

Many guests have been regulars here for years—some returning as many as 50 summers—although newcomers are made to feel just as welcome. "We like to see fresh faces here," comments caretaker Horst Taut. Standards in the restaurant are very high; a new menu every day offers from four to six entrées emphasizing seafood, and a full-time baker makes all the desserts, breads, and rolls. Thursday-night cookouts feature swordfish, steak, chicken, and seasonal vegetables.

The Weekapaug Inn is often described as a cruise ship on land or a summer camp—perhaps because it is an all-inclusive vacation spot with an American meal plan, card rooms, BYOB bars, lawn bowling, croquet, Ping-Pong, billiards, movies, and bingo nights. You also have access to a nearby golf course, a private beach, and tennis courts. Though many of its guests are middle-aged and older, the inn's children's program has made it a favorite of families, too. The full-time program director runs two daily sessions of special excursions and projects that make even the youngest guest feel welcome.

▦ *33 doubles with bath, 21 singles with bath. Restaurant. $165–$175; AP. No credit cards. No pets. 2-night minimum weekends, 3-night minimum holidays. Closed Labor Day–mid-June.*

Block Island

Hotel Manisses

Before the turn of the century, Block Island was touted as the Bermuda of the north. The beaches here are thick with sand; when conditions are right, the water is a Caribbean green; and, as in modern Bermuda, visitors on mopeds and bikes fill the roads. Situated 13 mi off the coast, Block Island is a very laid-back community. The local phone book lists numbers by just the last four digits (466 is the prefix), and you can dine at any of the island's finer restaurants in shorts and a T-shirt. This extraordinary nonchalance is exactly what a lot of vacationers are looking for. Most tourism here occurs between May and Columbus Day—at other times the majority of restaurants, inns, stores, and visitor services are closed.

In summer the population of 800 jumps to 10,000 on weekends; thousands come for just a day. Yet, thanks to the tireless efforts of local conservationists, the 11-square-mi island's beauty and privacy have been preserved; its 365 freshwater ponds make it a haven for more than 150 species of migrating birds, and its massive harbor is one of the cleanest in New England.

Block Island's original inhabitants were Native Americans, who called it Manisses, or Isle of the Little God. In 1524 the Italian explorer Giovanni da Verrazano renamed it Claudia, after the mother of the French king Francis I. In 1614 Dutch explorer Adrian Block renamed it after himself, and in 1661 the Massachusetts-claimed island was settled by 16 colonists who sought religious freedom; the farming and fishing community they established still exists. Old Harbor, where the ferries dock, is the island's main village, its streets lined with an eclectic collection of shops, restaurants, inns, and hotels.

Places to Go, Things to See

Although you can travel to Block Island by small plane (New England Airlines, tel. 800/243–2460), most folks arrive on ferries that cross Block Island Sound year-round from Galilee, Rhode Island, and in the summer from Providence and Newport as well as New London, Connecticut, and Montauk, New York. You don't need a car; most distances are easily covered on foot or by rented moped or bicycle, and taxis are readily available. Spring and fall here are just as appealing as summer; these extra-quiet shoulder seasons are popular with veteran Block Island visitors.

Animal Farm (Spring St.). The owners of the 1661 Inn and Hotel Manisses run a small farm with a collection of llamas, emus, sheep, goats, and ducks. There's no admission; just stop by to see (and pet) the animals.

Block Island Historical Cemetery. The views of the island from this graveyard on Job's Hill are stunning. Many tombstones dating from the 1700s bear family names still common to Block Island.

Block Island Historical Society (Old Town Rd., tel. 401/466–2481). Permanent and special exhibits of the society celebrate the island's farming and maritime past.

Clay Head Nature Trail. Pick up this walk at its subtly marked entrance on Corn Neck Road to explore an amazing 2-mi trail along ocean cliffs. Other trails head west through pine and scrub woodlands, an area called the Maze.

Mohegan Bluffs. Take Spring Street south out of the village to the Mohegan Trail, where—at the southern tip of the island—you'll find dramatic ocean views from a height of more than 350 ft. Stop inside the *Southeast Light* (tel. 401/466–5009), an 1873 brick building with gingerbread detailing. Here you'll learn about the successful grassroots campaign that moved the massive structure back from the receding cliffs.

The North Light. This lighthouse at Sandy Point, the northernmost tip of Block Island, was built in 1867 of Connecticut granite hauled to the site by oxen. It was restored recently and now houses exhibits on maritime history and birds. Watch out for the thousands of seagulls nesting in the rocks that lead up to the lighthouse.

Rodman's Hollow. Along Cooneymus Road, this is one of Block Island's five wildlife refuges. It is also a natural wonder—a ravine formed by a glacier. Many winding paths trace the deep, dramatic cleft all the way down to the ocean. In summer guided tours run a few times a week; look for announcements in the *Block Island Times.*

Beaches

Block Island is ringed with beaches, but the only one with a bathhouse and lifeguards is **Fred Benson Town Beach,** part of Crescent Beach, off Corn Neck Road. You'll find white sand at **Mansion Beach,** at the north end of Crescent Beach and the south of Clayhead Trail. For solitude try **Vail Beach,** on the south end of the island; take the path at the end of Snake Hollow Road.

Restaurants

Ballard's Inn (Old Harbor, tel. 401/466–2231) is a noisy, lively spot that caters to the boating crowd and serves drinks on a private beach. At **Finn's Seafood Bar** (Water St., tel. 401/466–2473) you can eat inside or on the deck with its panoramic view of the harbor. The smoked-bluefish pâté is wonderful. Sophisticated **Eli's** (Chapel St., tel. 401/466–5230) restaurant has a wide array of pasta dishes; portions here are large enough for two people to share (there's a $4 sharing charge, though). **G. R. Sharky's** (Corn Neck Rd., tel. 401/466–2249) has become a favorite spot with the locals. This newly rebuilt restaurant is open year-round and has a full bar, a children's menu, and an 8-ft hammerhead shark mounted on a wall.

Reservations Service

Block Island Holidays (Box 803, Block Island 02807, tel. 401/466–8855) offers group rates and package deals.

Visitor Information

Block Island Chamber of Commerce (Drawer D, Block Island 02807, tel. 401/466–2982).

Atlantic Inn

High St. (Box 1788), 02807, tel. 401/466–5883 or 800/224–7422

When the Clinton family visited Block Island in the summer of 1997, the president and his host, Senator Jack Reed, chose the Atlantic Inn for dinner. Locals knew that this choice was a good one. Innkeeper Brad Marthens and his wife, Anne, bought the inn in 1994. The two had vacationed on the island for years. "We both love the ocean, so this place is perfect for us," says Brad, who, in addition to hiring a talented staff, has greatly improved the inn's offerings and services.

Since 1879 this long, white Victorian with a blue gambrel roof has bravely fronted the elements from a hilltop overlooking the ocean. Big windows, high ceilings, and a sweeping staircase make the atmosphere open and breezy. The inn is furnished with turn-of-the-century pieces, many of them golden oak, which make it seem austere. This is softened by the pastel colors that are used throughout and the many homey and unusual touches: Witness the oak phone booth, just off the lobby, and the common bathroom, which has framed clips from old advertising campaigns. Guest rooms are spacious—though not huge—and have oak and maple furnishings, most of which are original to the building.

And then there are the views. Isolated from the hubbub of the Old Harbor area, here you can perch on a hillside and contemplate the shape of the island or the sparkle of nearby ocean. The inn's remarkable location makes it a popular place for weddings; many shoulder-season weekends are booked with nuptial celebrations.

A buffet breakfast with fresh-baked goods is prepared each morning by the inn's pastry chef. The restaurant, which is open for dinner May through October, serves four-course, prix-fixe meals. The 6-acre grounds are carefully maintained and have large wildflower, herb, and vegetable gardens (the produce of which is used in the kitchen). You'll also find two tennis courts and a smooth green croquet lawn.

🏨 *21 doubles with bath. Restaurant; phones, fans in rooms; games; books. $115–$210; Continental breakfast. D, MC, V. No smoking, no pets. 2- or 3-night minimum weekends June–Aug. Closed Nov.–Mar.*

Barrington Inn

Beach and Ocean Aves. (Box 397), 02807, tel. 401/466–5510

When a former Welcome Wagon hostess decides to open a B&B, you can bet she'll do things right. Owners Howard and Joan Ballard keep a tidy, inviting place. They enjoy helping you plan your days; the large breakfast table is commonly called "command central." Their innate hospitality is evident by how common it is to see Howard chauffeuring around guests in his 1915 Model-T Ford.

Joan and Howard completely restored this 1886 farmhouse after they bought it in 1982. It is furnished with a friendly assortment of antiques, some dating from the mid-19th century. You'll also find such eccentric decorations as a French hand-painted mirror—Joan's pride and joy. Meticulously clean, precisely arranged, and thoroughly soundproofed, the Barrington Inn is not recommended for children.

The homey, soundproofed B&B affords unusual views of Trims Pond, Great Salt Pond, and Crescent Beach. Four of the rooms have private decks (there's also a large common deck). Although the individual items aren't remarkable, the inn's mixed bag of antique furniture is unique because every piece was acquired on Block Island.

🏨 *6 doubles with bath, 2 apartments. Ceiling fans in rooms, TV/VCR in common room. $105–$149; Continental breakfast. MC, V. No smoking, no pets. Closed Dec.–Mar.*

Blue Dory Inn

Dodge St. (Box 488), 02807, tel. 401/466–5891 or 800/992–7290, fax 401/466–9910

Located in the Old Harbor historic district, the Blue Dory Inn has been a guest house since its construction in 1898 by Brunell Dodge, a Block Island fisherman. Dodge was also an artist; an example of his wood-burning skills hangs over the doorway of the inn's Victorian-style parlor, which is furnished with floral wallpaper and a curved sofa. Hors d'oeuvres, wine, and home-baked cookies are served here every afternoon.

Thanks to Ann Loedy, the dynamic owner-manager, things in the main building and the three small shingle-and-clapboard outbuildings run efficiently. Guest rooms are not large, but each is tastefully appointed and has either an ocean or a harbor view. Couples looking for a romantic hideaway often enjoy the Tea House, with its porch that overlooks Crescent Beach. There's a small, cozy living room, and an expanded Continental breakfast is served each morning in a homey kitchen that faces the ocean.

▦ *13 doubles with bath, 4 suites, 3 cottages. Cable TV in lobby. $135–$350; Continental breakfast. AE, D, MC, V. No smoking. 2-night minimum weekends.*

Hotel Manisses

1 Spring St., 02807, tel. 401/466–2063 or 800/626–4773, fax 401/466–3162

If you were to stroll along Spring Street on a foggy night, your eye might be caught by a translucent glow in the sky. Continue down the street, and you'll discover the source: the magnificent brass chandelier—a beacon of welcome from a bygone era—suspended inside the cupola of the Manisses.

This 1870 Victorian inn has been restored with loving care and is now diligently maintained by its owners and operators—Joan and Justin Abrams, their daughter Rita Draper, and her husband, Steve. (The family also owns and operates the nearby 1661 Inn & Guest House; *see below*.) No expense was spared in the renovation and decoration, but what's perhaps more important, the Draper and Abrams families work hard to make you feel comfortable and pampered. Indeed, they have made attention to detail an art form; staff members dressed in ties or Victorian-era dresses are kept remarkably busy.

You can enjoy such unique offerings as afternoon wine and "nibblets" in the romantic parlor that overlooks the garden, coffee and tea available throughout the day, picnic baskets packed with lunch, guided tours of the island, and an animal farm with llamas and emus.

Furnishings were chosen with care. Many of the guest rooms, named after famous shipwrecks, are filled with intriguing knickknacks and unusual Victorian pieces, such as the many-leveled bureau in the Princess Augusta Room and an ivory toilet set on a bureau in another. (Note that because of all the antiques, this inn is not suitable for children.) Bedside decanters and bowls of candy are among the thoughtful touches, and some rooms have large hot tubs. The Manisses's restaurant, on the lower level, is considered one of Rhode Island's best and features vegetables grown in the inn's garden, local seafood, and homemade bread.

More economical accommodations are available down the road at Dodge Cottage. Although not as grand as accommodations at the Manisses, the cottage has a large common room and the cozy feel of a small B&B. A large breakfast is served at the 1661 Inn, a five-minute walk up the road. This buffet of eggs, sausage, cornbread, smoked bluefish, muffins, and much more is popular with guests and walk-ins alike.

▦ *17 doubles with bath. Restaurant; phones, ceiling fans in rooms; whirlpool baths in some rooms; petting farm. $146–$255; buffet breakfast served at nearby inn. AE, MC, V.*

Rose Farm Inn

Roslyn Rd. (Box E), 02807, tel. 401/466–2034, fax 401/466–2021

Judy and Robert Rose were born and raised on Block Island. In 1988 they restored the house built by Robert's grandfather at the turn of the century. A second building, the Captain Rose House, was added in 1993. Its nine new rooms are furnished with antiques but also have such modern amenities as whirlpool baths and decks.

Each of the pleasantly uncluttered rooms at the Rose Farm Inn offers bucolic views—some of the ocean, some of nearby ponds. The furnishings are a combination of antiques and high-quality reproductions. Of the turn-of-the-century walnut bed in one room, Judy says proudly, "Golden oak was common at that time. Walnut was very *unusual.* Look at the beautiful grain in that piece!" Another intriguing item is a Victorian ladies' hotel bureau, with a special compartment for hats and gloves.

The breakfast room is furnished in wicker and decorated with hanging plants, and a spacious front porch makes a perfect setting for reflective moments. The grown-up, sometimes-romantic atmosphere of the Rose Farm Inn makes this an inappropriate place for children.

🏨 *17 doubles with bath, 2 doubles share bath. Cable TV in common room; refrigerator, ice machine available. $95–$179; Continental breakfast. AE, D, MC, V. No smoking. 3-night minimum July–Aug., 2-night minimum weekends June and Sept.–Oct.*

The 1661 Inn & Guest House

Spring St., 02807, tel. 401/466–2421, 401/466–2063, or 800/626–4773, fax 401/466–2858

If your island vacation fantasy includes lounging in bed while gazing at swans in the marshes that overlook the blue Atlantic, consider booking a room at the 1661 Inn. Owners Joan and Justin Abrams and operators Rita and Steve Draper (*see* Hotel Manisses, *above*) are noted for their attention to detail. Even if your room doesn't face the water, you can loll on the inn's expansive deck or curl up in a chair on the gently sloping oceanside lawn; from both spots you'll enjoy the panorama of the water below.

In the front hallway a wall full of pictures of the inn taken by former guests attests to how special a stay here has been for many people. Although recent refurbishments reduced the number of guest rooms, those that remain have been enlarged and given luxurious appointments. Many rooms offer whirlpool baths, often accompanied by Victorian fainting couches that allow the whirlpool-induced glow to linger. Room decor reflects the innkeepers' attention to detail: floral wallpaper in one room matches the colors of the hand-painted tiles atop its antique bureau; another room has a collection of handmade wooden model ships; and a suite that faces the ocean has an antique canopy bed.

Breakfast is a splendid experience, particularly in summer when it's served on the deck. The ample buffet may consist of fresh bluefish, corned-beef hash, Boston baked beans, sausage, Belgian waffles, roasted potatoes, French toast, scrambled eggs, hot and cold cereal, fruit juices, and fresh muffins. Afternoon cocktails are served down the street at the Hotel Manisses and include such hors d'oeuvres as bluefish pâté and superspicy nachos.

Adjacent to the inn is the Nicholas Ball Cottage, with smaller rooms and some shared baths. Though lodgings here are slightly more spartan, the prices are quite reasonable, and all the inn's amenities remain available.

🏨 *9 doubles with bath in inn; 5 doubles with bath, 4 doubles share bath in guest house. Phones in rooms, 4 wheelchair-accessible rooms. $60–$325; full buffet breakfast. AE, MC, V. No pets.*

Surf Hotel

Dodge St. (Box C), 02807, tel. 401/466–2241

The Cyrs—Beatrice, Ulric, and Lorraine—have operated the Surf Hotel since 1956. A stone's throw from the ferry dock, in the heart of the Old Harbor area and near Crescent Beach, the hotel seems to have changed very little over the years; in fact, it's not hard to imagine what the hotel must have been like when it first opened in 1876. Dimly lighted hallways take you to small, tidy guest rooms furnished with a jumble of antique furniture and odds and ends. The dining room's ceiling is the original tin. In the parlor you'll find Victorian curios, such as a perambulator stuffed with 1890s baby dolls—each with a startled expression. You can watch the town go by or the crashing of the waves from one of the 30 high-backed rockers on the front porch.

The guest rooms have their own sinks but share toilets and baths—as Lorraine points out, when the building was constructed, bathrooms were rare—but return guests (and there are *many* of them) don't seem to mind sharing.

🏨 *34 doubles and 1 single share 9 baths. Barbecue grill, beach towels, chairs, umbrellas, children's play area, picnic tables. $70–$130; Continental-plus breakfast. MC, V. No pets. 6-night minimum July–Aug. Closed Columbus Day–Memorial Day.*

Massachusetts

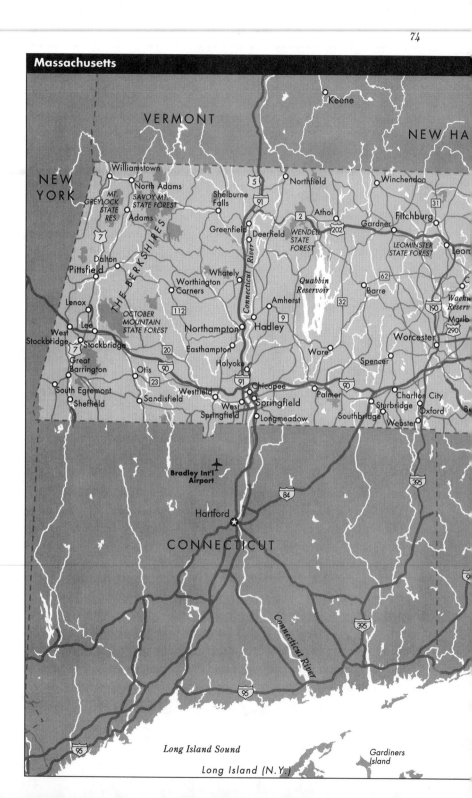

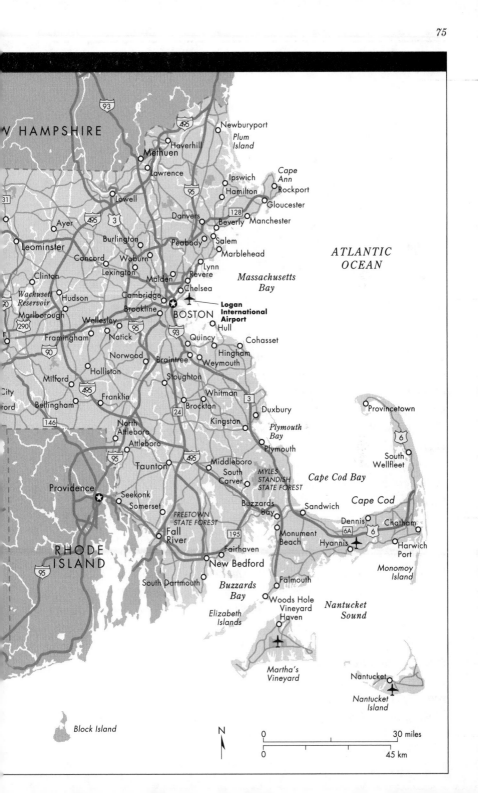

Southeastern Massachusetts

Jackson-Russell-Whitfield House

Travelers often zip through southeastern Massachusetts (dubbed the South Coast) on their way elsewhere—usually, Cape Cod. Yet this region offers many surprises and far fewer Winnebagos and tour buses (except, perhaps, around Plymouth Rock) than other parts of the state. You can reach Quincy, the birthplace of presidents John Adams and John Quincy Adams, via Route 3 and the meandering roads closer to the coast. Farther south and over to Route 3A, you'll pass through the seaside towns of Hingham, Cohasset, Greenbush, and Marshfield. Several public beaches are also accessible down side roads. A little farther south, you can enjoy the storybook town of Duxbury, first settled in the 17th century by the Pilgrims soon after they arrived in Plymouth. You can rejoin Route 3 just outside Duxbury or continue south on 3A to Kingston, another Pilgrim settlement, and 4 mi beyond that to Plymouth.

If you head south from Boston on Route 24, you'll arrive at Fall River and New Bedford in about an hour. Both cities reached peak prosperity in the 19th century, and both have restored buildings of that era—often housing antiques and

outlet stores. Boats from New Bedford Harbor depart each day
for Martha's Vineyard and Cuttyhunk Island.

Places to Go, Sights to See

Fall River. Industrial docks and enormous factories hark back to the city's
past as a major textile center. It also served as a port, however, and its most
interesting site is *Battleship Cove* (access from I–195, exit 5, beside the Taunton
River, tel. 508/678–1100), which harbors several museums, the 35,000-ton World
War II battleship USS *Massachusetts*, the destroyer USS *Kennedy*, and the
attack sub USS *Lionfish*. The *Marine Museum at Fall River* (70 Water St., tel.
508/674–3533) displays ship models, steam engines, and memorabilia from the
Titanic and the Old Fall River Line. The *Fall River Historical Society* (451 Rock
St., tel. 508/679–1071) is housed in an 1843 Greek Revival house that was built of
Fall River granite. Period antiques and furnishings fill the 16 rooms, many of
which are open to the public (call for tour times). The society is also home to a
small but fascinating collection of memorabilia documenting the trial of Lizzie
Borden, who was accused of chopping her father and stepmother to death in
August 1892.

New Bedford. Home of the largest fishing fleet on the east coast, this former
whaling capital has a delightful historic district. While wandering its cobblestone
streets near the waterfront, you can shop for antiques and boating supplies.
In this district the 1834 Greek Revival residence of a whaling merchant is
now the *Rotch-Jones-Duff House and Garden Museum* (396 County St., tel.
508/997–1401). At the *New Bedford Whaling Museum* (18 Johnny Cake Hill, tel.
508/997–0046), exhibits include a model of the square-rigger *Lagoda*, a superb
collection of scrimshaw, a number of whaling journals, and a huge selection of
whaling gear. *Seamen's Bethel* (15 Johnny Cake Hill, no phone) is a 19th-century
chapel that was immortalized at the beginning of Herman Melville's *Moby Dick*.
The pew in which Melville sat is marked with a plaque, and memorials to lost
seamen line the walls. The Bethel—still in use today—also has a pulpit shaped
like a whaling boat's bow.

Plymouth. This pleasant residential and industrial community with steep
streets leading down to the harbor cherishes its history as the site of Plymouth
Colony, the first permanent New England settlement, established by the English
Pilgrims in the 17th century. Don't miss *Plymouth Rock:* The oversize boulder
with a granite enclosure at water's edge is traditionally accepted as the initial
landing spot of the Pilgrims, who disembarked from the *Mayflower* in 1620. You
can also visit the *Mayflower II* (State Pier, tel. 508/746–1622), a replica of what
the original Pilgrim ship probably looked like (no one is quite sure). *Plimoth
Plantation* (137 Warren Ave., Rte. 3A, 3 mi south of Plymouth, tel. 508/746–1622),
a reconstruction of a 1627 Pilgrim village, has furnished, thatched-roof, wooden
homes; gardens; roaming animals; and villagers in period dress demonstrating
household skills. Everything is authentic—ask the folks portraying the villagers
a question, and they'll answer you in Olde English, provided it's a question about
events prior to the 17th century!

South Dartmouth. The *Children's Museum* (276 Gulf Rd., tel. 508/993–3361), housed in a former dairy barn on 60 acres of land, has a hand-carved saltwater aquarium, a hands-on miniature village, a teddy bear collection, an energy exhibition, hiking trails, maple-sugaring tours in March, and more. A stop at *Salvadore's Ice Cream* (Smith Neck Rd., no phone) is a must—the frozen treats are homemade, and the building is in the shape of an enormous black milk can.

Beaches

Several South Shore and Buzzards Bay beaches are under the jurisdictions of the towns in which they're located; watch for local parking regulations. State beaches in the area include **Demarest Lloyd State Park** in Dartmouth, **Fort Phoenix State Beach** in Fairhaven, **Horseneck Beach** in Westport, and **Nantasket Beach** in Hull.

Restaurants

In New Bedford, **Candleworks Restaurant** (72 N. Water St., tel. 508/997–1294) serves well-prepared seafood on the ground floor of a beautifully restored Federal-style candle factory. **Freestone's City Grill** (41 William St., tel. 508/993–7477), also in New Bedford, is in an 1877 bank building and offers classic American, international, and vegetarian fare. In South Dartmouth the **Bridge Street Café** (10A Bridge St., tel. 508/994–7200) has tasty fish dishes as well as a casual bistro menu in a quaint harborside setting. **Crane Brook Tea Room** (229 Fremont St., tel. 508/866–3235), in Carver, serves fine French-influenced fare in an antiques-filled spot set at the edge of a pond.

Reservations Service

New England Hospitality Network (Box 3291, Newport, RI 02840, tel. 401/849–1298 or 800/828–0000).

Visitor Information

Coastal South Shore information is handled by the **Plymouth County Development Council** (Box 1620, Pembroke 02359, tel. 781/826–3136). For New Bedford and Fall River information, try the **Bristol County Convention and Visitors Bureau** (70 N. 2nd St., New Bedford 02740, tel. 508/997–1250 or 800/288–6263).

Edgewater
Bed and Breakfast

2 Oxford St., Fairhaven 02719, tel. 508/ 997–5512, fax 508/997–5784

When *Star Trek* star Patrick Stewart visited the New Bedford Whaling Museum to do research for a film based on *Moby Dick*, he stayed here. It's a good choice. Overlooking New Bedford Harbor on the grassy slopes of the ironically named Poverty Point, it's hard to believe that this cedar-shingled B&B is a mere five minutes' drive from I–195.

There are six rooms in the main 1880 house, all with cable TV, tasteful period furnishings, and private baths (two with original claw-foot tubs); four rooms have water views. The Captain's Suite—the room in which Stewart stayed—has a fireplace and lead-glass details; the views of New Bedford Harbor are so magnificent you'll swear you were standing on the bow of a ship. There are two rooms on the first floor of the older (1760) portion of the house; on top is the Joshua Slocum Suite, a quaint one-bedroom gem, with a fully furnished kitchen, a deck, and a living room with a fireplace.

Owner Kathy Reed, a part-time college professor, has run the Edgewater since April 1984 and has worked hard to refurbish and remodel. The earth-tone sunken living room (check out the original dental moldings and wave-glass windows) has a fireplace and overstuffed chairs and a sofa that make taking in the water views a pastime that approaches meditation. (Indeed, this inn's atmosphere makes it unsuitable for very young children.)

Kathy goes out of her way to make sure you have everything, but she's smart enough to know when you want to be alone. Looking for a great restaurant? Kathy has the menus. Can't get into that restaurant? Kathy will pull some strings. Need help planning a day trip? If Kathy doesn't have the information, she'll get

it for you. You can map out your day over a Continental-plus breakfast in the formal water-view dining room. Before heading out, be sure to meander through the gardens (if the lilacs are in bloom, stop for a sniff) or daydream for a bit in one of the chairs at the water's edge.

🏠 *4 doubles with bath, 1 suite, 1 efficiency. TVs and phones in rooms. $65– $85; Continental-plus breakfast. AE, D, MC, V. No smoking in common area, no pets. 2-night minimum weekends and holidays in peak season.*

Foxglove Cottage

101 Sandwich Rd., Plymouth 02360, tel. 508/747–6576 or 800/479–4746, fax 508/ 747–7622

Foxglove Cottage is just a few miles from downtown Plymouth on winding, tree-lined Sandwich Road—the original Colonial highway to Boston. Just look for the house painted pink, a color favored inside, too. Set on 40 acres of rolling fields and woods, the cottage has a spacious lawn bordered by holly, rhododendrons, and the remnants of an old stone wall. The front of the inn, an 1820 Cape-style clapboard home, faces a pasture with horses; the gravel drive and entrance are at the side. You enter the inn through the cheerful Common Room, a 1950s addition furnished with a geranium-print sofa and chairs, green wall-to-wall carpeting, a fireplace, and a late-Victorian oak rocking chair, chest, and armoire, which holds a TV and VCR.

Michael Cowan and her husband, Charlie, bought the house in 1990, and their love for European B&Bs led them to convert it to an inn. They removed shingles to restore the original clapboard look, exposed wide-board floors once hidden in attic space, and meticulously furnished each room with matching antiques.

Michael favors the Victorian period, and every room in the original house is carefully decorated with coordinating fabrics, wallpapers, and collectibles—some of which are for sale. Lamps, tea sets, and china dogs and cats are set on tables; portraits of women on ivory and porcelain hang on the walls. (Owing to the number of antiques and breakables, it's best to leave your little ones at home.)

The first-floor Rose Room has a fishnet canopied bed, a Victorian settee, rose-patterned wallpaper, a collection of antique chocolate pots, and a private bath with shower. The second-floor quarters, the Marble Room and Canopy Room, are on either side of a landing. Each has beautiful wide-board floors, an English gas fireplace, two upholstered chairs with a lamp between them, and a private bath with tub and shower. The Marble Room has a rose and cream paisley comforter on the bed and English floral wallpaper in the colors of lettuce green, lavender, rose, and grape. There are a needlepoint chair, needlepoint pillows on the bed, and a marble-top walnut dresser with a Palladian mirror. The Canopy Room features a bed with white-eyelet comforter and pillows. Framed silhouettes on the wall pick up on the black trim of the fabrics and rose wallpaper.

A full breakfast—perhaps waffles with bananas and maple syrup or a sausage, egg, and cheese casserole—is served in the small, formal dining room in front of a fireplace with an original beehive oven. In good weather it's served on the deck off the Common Room.

🎏 *3 doubles with bath. Air-conditioning, TV/VCR and minirefrigerator in common room, bicycles, croquet. $75– $95; full breakfast. D. No smoking, no pets. 2-night minimum weekends and holidays in peak season.*

Jackson-Russell-Whitfield House

26 North St., Plymouth 02360, tel. 508/ 746–5289, fax 508/747–2722

Don't judge a book—or a B&B—by its cover. In the middle of town, steps from Plymouth Rock, the 1782 Jackson-Russell-Whitfield House needs an exterior face-lift. But get past the rickety fence, peeling paint, and unkempt front yard, and you'll find an inviting interior. Dr. Brian Whitfield originally bought the house in 1987 for his chiropractic practice, but then decided it was too nice for an office. He's the first owner unrelated to Samuel Jackson, the ship captain and banker who built it.

The elegant common areas are furnished as if still occupied by the original owners, who profited from Asian and European trade. The living room has inviting stuffed chairs and a comfortable sofa, a 17th-century Japanese screen, a velvet ottoman, an Asian carpet in deep pinks and blues, an aubergine velvet armchair, and a Chippendale sideboard with a decanter of spirits. Chinese portraits on scrolls frame the doorway to the music room, which houses a 1917 Steinway baby grand piano, gleaming against the deep green walls. Throughout are quarter-cut oak parquet floors and fluted moldings dating from 1847. (Parents take note: young children may not fully appreciate—or respect—all the collectibles here, though teenagers might.)

Upstairs, the Blue Room has large windows and Asian carpets. Russian blue trim and wainscoting match the floral wallpaper, whose stylized birds complement the Spice Islands carving of the four-poster bed. There are tiger-maple night tables with lamps on either side of the bed, and the room also has a working fireplace. Mirror-paned doors open to the adjoining Stenciled Room, where contemporary artist Carolyn Hedge has painted willow and other traditional motifs. This room has two four-poster twin beds with white spreads, ivory drapes, and a tiger-maple dresser and night table. There is one bath for both rooms, but the two rooms are only rented together. Next door is a room whose walls are entirely covered in murals of serene pale green trees and pastures overlooking a harbor. A row of teddy bears sits on the 1810 walnut four-poster canopy bed. Brian's mother, Phyllis, lives in this room during the summer, when she flies in from California to run the inn.

When in residence, Phyllis presides over breakfast—baking scones, muffins, and a much-requested streusel coffee cake—served in the comfortably formal dining room with its 19th-century crystal chandelier and its mural of hand-painted clouds on the ceiling. In the off-season, Brian tends to guests in the afternoon and evening, and his friend Jay Hall bakes and serves breakfast.

🏠 *2 doubles share bath in summer (another double, which shares bath, is available in winter). Air-conditioning. $80–140; Continental-plus breakfast. MC, V. No smoking, no pets, 2-night minimum weekends and holidays in peak season.*

The Little Red House

631 Elm St., South Dartmouth 02748, tel. 508/996–4554

The outside may be red, but you'll be tickled pink by the relaxing, welcoming intimacy of the rooms. Owner Meryl Zwirblis only rents two of her three second-floor rooms at any one time, assuring solitude (this inn is not suitable for young children) and personal service.

The rooms are appointed with antiques; have twin, full, or queen-size beds; and share a decidedly feminine pink bath, complete with plush terry-cloth robes. The Heart Room is especially charming, with its ultrasoft four-poster queen-size bed and its delightful heartfelt touches. Meryl has tucked heart-shaped accessories and doodads *everywhere*, yet the gimmick is so well done that it accentuates—and never cheapens—the decor. For the last 10 years, Meryl has been running a contest: Guess the number of heart-shaped objects in the room, and she'll give you a glorious wall hanging. But be forewarned: To date, only one couple has answered correctly, and that's because, Meryl points out, they stayed in the room for a week!

At the end of a summer's day, nothing beats gazing at the neighbor's cows as you relax in the garden gazebo . . . except, maybe, savoring sherry in front of the fireplace in the rose-motif living room.

🏠 *2 doubles share bath. TV in common room. $60–$75; full breakfast, afternoon tea. No credit cards. No smoking, no pets.*

Lizzie Borden Bed and Breakfast

92 2nd St., Fall River 02721, tel. and fax 508/675–7333

Here you can get 40 winks while dreaming about the 40 whacks Lizzie Borden (supposedly) gave her father and stepmother back on August 4, 1892. The Greek Revival house—erected in 1845 and until 1996 a private residence—has been turned into the city's most quixotic sightseeing spot. Borden buffs, true-crime fans, and the curious flock here to sleep, snoop, and have their photos taken in the exact spots where the bodies were found.

The six rooms are small but cozy and have double beds; four rooms share baths. Each has been faithfully restored to look the same way it did on that fateful August day, and all but the three attic rooms are named for a Borden family member. The rooms all have Borden family-member portraits, Borden memorabilia, and a diary in which guests leave thoughts. (Young children may not appreciate the theme or the museum-like atmosphere here.)

The Lizzie and Emma Suite (formerly Lizzie and Emma's bedrooms) has the green silk dress that actress Elizabeth Montgomery wore when she played Lizzie in a TV movie. It doesn't take a detective to figure out that the most popular room is the John Morse Guest Room, named for Lizzie's uncle and the one in which stepmom Abby was found hacked to death. (Those wanting to spend August 4 in this room should reserve early; it's usually booked a year in advance.) Breakfast—bananas, johnnycakes, sugar cookies, and coffee—is similar to the last one the Bordens ate. And don't forget to check out the framed hatchet hanging on the kitchen wall; it was found in a closet during a 1948 renovation; police investigations have determined it was not the murder weapon.

If you'd rather not spend the night, you can just take one of the nine daily tours led by knowledgeable guides in Victorian garb. They begin in the first-floor sitting room, where Andrew was murdered. (Those dying for more morbidity should check out the grisly crime-scene photo on the wall.) The sitting room has a video and book lending library and sundry souvenirs for sale. So did Lizzie—who was tried and acquitted of the crimes—do it? Says B&B co-owner Ron Evans with a smile: "We let the guests make up their own minds."

🏠 *2 doubles with bath, 4 doubles share bath, 1 suite. Air-conditioning. $150–$200; full breakfast, tour. AE, D, MC, V. No smoking, no pets.*

Onset Pointe Inn

9 Eagle Way (Box 1450), Onset 02558, tel. 508/295-8442 or 800/356-6738, fax 508/295-5241

Looking for a seaside resort with all the charm (and romance) of Cape Cod that's off the beaten track? Look no farther. Situated on Pointe Independence, a spit of land in Buzzards Bay near the entrance to the Cape Cod Canal, this Victorian mansion (circa 1880) offers a prized proximity: the marina and private beach are just a few footprints in the sand away.

The seven main-house rooms are furnished in a typical, yet tasteful, seaside resort way: wicker and chintz, and lots of it. Two second-floor rooms have private balconies; the largest room, Bay View, is on the turreted third floor and

offers panoramic water views of Onset Marina and Buzzards Bay and spectacular sunsets. In addition to the main house, you'll also find a guest house with five quarters (two suites that have kitchens and three rooms that sleep at least three people); a carriage house with two suites (one with a kitchen and one without); and one fully furnished apartment. (Families traveling with children should be sure to book a room in the guest house or the carriage house—where everyone will be most comfortable.)

The sun-drenched, glass-walled common room is replete with TV, stereo, fireplace, and myriad puzzles and games. It's also easy to while away your time in an Adirondack chair on one of the inn's many porches. Breakfast is served in the equally stunning, flagstone, ivy-trimmed sunporch.

🏠 *7 doubles with bath, 3 triples with bath, 4 suites, 1 apartment. Phones in main building rooms, beach access, volleyball. $85–$150; Continental-plus breakfast for main-building guests. AE, D, MC, V. No smoking, no pets. 2-night minimum weekends and holidays in peak season.*

Salt Marsh Farm

322 Smith Neck Rd., South Dartmouth 02748, tel. 508/992-0980

Located on the historic Isaac Howland homestead farm at the quiet end of a harborside road in South Dartmouth, this two-story, mint-condition Georgian farmhouse (circa 1770) is run by Sally and Larry Brownell and has been in Sally's family since World War II. In the back of the house lie 90 acres of grounds, where nature trails lead to maples, oaks, and hollies; a 30-acre salt marsh; and the sparkling waters of Little River.

The Brownells have turned over the front of their home to guests, who may lounge by the fireplace in the living room filled with books on local nature lore and history. A large gallery-type family room, where you'll probably see jigsaw puzzles laid out, runs the length of the house. The building is full of pewter, silver, and choice antiques—virtually all passed down through Sally's or Larry's families. Some of the pieces date back generations, such as the massive mahogany sideboard in the intimate dining room, where portraits of four of Sally's Colonial ancestors gaze down on the scene.

Each of the two guest rooms has its own hall and stairway; one has twin four-poster beds and the other a double bed. Handmade quilts cover the beds, and freshly picked flowers decorate the rooms. On the wall in the Rocking Horse Room is an unusual picture of a parrot made entirely of feathers. One of the bathrooms has an oversize, claw-foot tub and a tub-height window with a view of the grounds.

Sally is an accomplished cook who makes good use of her organic herb and vegetable gardens. Her breakfast repertoire includes five-grain pancakes, fresh eggs (from the Brownell's henhouse) prepared in a number of ways, prize-winning blueberry muffins, and double-dipped French toast that's sometimes served with a special orange sauce and what Sally calls "mystery" syrup—made from rhubarb.

The town beach is within biking distance, and New Bedford is about 6 mi away. Padanaram, the name of the local harbor village, is used on many signposts.

▥ *2 doubles with bath. TV and phone in common area, bicycles (including one built for 2), nature trails. $75–$90; full breakfast, afternoon tea. MC, V. No smoking, no pets, children allowed but only if a separate room is rented for them. 2-night minimum weekends in peak season and holidays.*

The Saltworks

115 Elm St., South Dartmouth 02748, tel. 508/991–5491, fax 508/979–8470

On what was once the grounds of an 1840 saltworks now sits a posh—but hardly pretentious—B&B, tucked away inside a private gated community. David Hall, a boat restorer, and his wife, Sandra, opened the Saltworks in 1995, mixing new and old with unsurpassed finesse.

There are only two rooms, each a suite with private bath and a working fireplace. The South Suite has a stunning 1895 Simmons brass bed that will offer you the best sleep you've had in years (best to leave the kids at home); the bath has an original claw-foot tub, a marble sink, and pine-plank floors that are painted red.

The large, airy common room has a TV, a fireplace, and enough reading material to keep a bibliophile busy for days—grab your favorite prose and cozy up in the window seat. The wraparound porch—crammed with nautical touches such as a lobster-trap-cum-table—offers panoramic views of Padanaram Harbor. A short walk will take you to Padanaram Village—that is, *if* you want to leave.

▥ *2 suites. TV in common room, beach access. $85; Continental-plus breakfast. AE, MC, V. No smoking, no pets. 2-night minimum weekends and holidays in peak season. Closed mid-Dec.–mid-Jan.*

Sconehedge

280 Sandwich St., Plymouth 02360, tel. 508/746–1847, fax 508/746–3736

At first glance this large, cedar-shingle, 1910 mansion (no other word will do) is unpretentious and plain. Then the massive oak doors open and . . . well, think back to when Dorothy landed in Oz, and everything turned from sepia to Technicolor. But remember: This is real—not reel—life.

With its formal, dark poplar-beamed entrance hall (covered in muted, moss-green, swan-motif wallpaper), its ornate staircase, its diamond-pane windows, and its whimsical pierced-copper-and-glass light fixtures made by owner David Berman, Sconehedge seems to have been decorated—at least in part—by Charles Addams *and* Edward Gorey . . . perhaps even Norman Bates. Berman—who bought the dilapidated house in 1994 and spent 10 months restoring it—is an expert on the English designer-architect Charles Voysey, and every room is enriched with faithful reproductions of Voysey's designs, from wallpaper to clocks to curtains. This is a house where Victorian and Edwardian meld with Arts and Crafts, Gothic, even a little Berman. How else could you explain the odd pieces of taxidermy here and there?

There are three rooms and one suite, all with hand-painted furniture (yet another of Berman's talents) that seem plucked from the pages of turn-of-the-century fairy tales, four-poster or antique brass beds, private baths, and fireplaces. The second-floor suite, which has a sunporch that overlooks the gardens, is perhaps the most spectacular. It is connected to the Alice in Wonderland Room, so named because its wallpaper features Lewis Carroll's characters.

Why Sconehedge? Friends came up with the name because of Berman's love for baking classic English scones. You'll find out at breakfast just how good they are; *almost* as delicious as the house itself.

🏠 *3 doubles with bath, 1 suite. Air-conditioning, TV in common area, croquet. $95–$165; full breakfast. MC, V. No*

smoking, no pets. 2-night minimum weekends, 3-night minimum holidays.

The Windsor House

390 Washington St., Duxbury 02332, tel. 781/934–0991 or 800/934–0993, fax 781/ 934–5955

The large white building that houses this inn was built in 1803 by Nathaniel Windsor, a merchant sea captain. Three upstairs rooms are named for their color schemes and feature fireplaces and Colonial-style reproduction furniture. The Brown Room has a queen-size canopy bed; the Green Room has twin canopy beds and a bath down the hall. The larger Blue Room has twin beds and a pullout couch in a small adjoining room.

Downstairs you can relax in an English-style pub built in the 1930s with wood from a Pilgrim-period church next door. The pub benches were church pews. The carriage house restaurant opens onto a patio at lunchtime, and the more formal main dining room has post-and-beam construction. The specialty is fresh seafood (the grilled swordfish scampi is popular).

Owner David O'Connell is a hotelier who knows how to make you feel at home. You can walk to a beach and golf, tennis, swimming, and cross-country skiing are all nearby.

🏠 *3 doubles with bath. 2 restaurants, pub. $95–$135, $25 additional for each extra adult, $10 additional for each child under 16; full breakfast. AE, D, MC, V. No smoking, no pets.*

Cape Cod

Captain Freeman Inn

Traditionally associated with quaint villages, weathered-shingle cottages, dune-backed beaches, fog-enshrouded lighthouses, and clam chowder, the Cape has become so popular that it risks losing the charm that brought everyone here in the first place. More and more open land has been lost to housing developments and strip malls. In summer you really have to seek out tranquillity. Yet peace can still be found; much of the Cape remains compellingly beautiful, and always there is the sea.

Situated 60 mi southeast of Boston and separated from the rest of Massachusetts by the 17½-mi Cape Cod Canal, this craggy peninsula juts 70 mi into the ocean and looks like an arm bent at the elbow, its fist turned toward the mainland at Provincetown. The moderate coastal climate fosters an abundance of plant and animal life. Barrier beaches attract a stunning variety of shore and sea birds, and the marshes and ponds are rich in waterfowl. Gerry Studds Stellwagen Bank National Marine Sanctuary, just north of Provincetown, is a prime feeding ground for whales and dolphins; sandbars are playgrounds for harbor seals. Nature preserves laced with walking and bicycling trails encompass pine forests, marshes,

*swamps, and cranberry bogs. Across dunes anchored by
sturdy poverty grass sprawl beach plums, pink salt-spray
roses, and purple beach peas.*

*A less happy result of the Cape's coastal location is that, on
the Atlantic side especially, the tides regularly eat away at the
land, sometimes at an alarming rate. Many lighthouses, some
built hundreds of feet from the water's edge, have fallen into
the sea, and others are now in danger of being lost. In the
mid-19th century, Henry David Thoreau described the coast
here as "the edge of a continent wasting before the assaults
of the ocean." Thanks to the establishment of the Cape Cod
National Seashore in 1961, you can still walk almost 30 mi
of Atlantic beach without seeing a trace of humanity.*

*Through the creation of national historic districts, similar
protection has been extended to the Cape's man-made
landscapes. The largest and most pleasing is along the Old
King's Highway (Route 6A), where the Cape's first towns—
Sandwich, Barnstable, and Yarmouth—were settled by 1639.
Lining this tree-shaded country road, which traverses the
entire north shore, are early saltboxes, fancier houses built
later by prosperous sea captains, and traditional cottages—
shingles weathered to a silvery gray, with soft pink roses
spilling across them. Here, too, are the white steepled churches,
taverns, and village greens that preserve the spirit of old New
England, along with some of the Cape's many surviving
windmills.*

*Most villages have their own small museums, often set in
houses that are themselves historic. Borning and keeping
rooms, summer and winter kitchens, beehive ovens, a spinning
wheel, a stereopticon, a hand-stitched sampler, and other
remnants of the past tell tales of the English settlers and their
descendants. The travels of whaling and packet-schooner
seamen and captains in the area are recounted through
antique nautical equipment, harpoons, charts, maps, journals,
scrimshaw, and gifts brought back from exotic ports.*

Today the Cape depends on tourism, and there is a plethora of services and entertainment, including amusements for children. In addition to traditional clambakes—with lobsters, steamers, corn on the cob, baked potatoes, and maybe linguiça for a touch of the Cape's Portuguese flavor—eating places range from fried-clam shacks and rustic fish houses to elegant restaurants. Shoppers find no end of crafts and antiques stores and art galleries; theater buffs choose from many good community groups and college and professional summer stock troupes. Of course there are plenty of water sports, and everywhere there are bay and sound beaches—calm or wild, dune- or forest-backed, blanket-covered or secluded.

The "season" used to be strictly from Memorial Day to Labor Day, but many places now open in April or earlier and close as late as November; a core remain open year-round. Unfortunately, most of the historic sites and museums, largely manned by volunteers, still adhere to the traditional dates and are inaccessible in the off-season.

Each season invites a different kind of visit. In summer you can relax on a beach or fill your schedule with museum visits and other activities. In fall the crowds thin, the prices drop, and the water remains warm enough for swimming. Gently turning foliage reaches its peak in late October, with areas around the freshwater marshes, ponds, and swamps offering the brightest displays. Fall and winter are oyster and scallop season, and all the restaurants that are still open feature the freshly harvested delicacies. In the winter many tourist-oriented activities and facilities shut down, but accommodations (including fireplace-warmed inns) go for as little as half the summer rates, and you can walk the beaches in solitude. Spring is a bit wet, but the Cape is remarkable when the daffodils come bursting up and everything begins to turn green. By April shops and restaurants start to open, and locals begin to prepare for another summer.

Places to Go, Sights to See

Band Concerts. Every town has these slices of Americana. Chatham has particularly lively and popular concerts, held on Friday evening during the summer at *Kate Gould Park* (tel. 508/945–5199) on Main Street; as many as 6,000 people show up, and hundreds of them will spend the night on the dance floor. There are also special dances for children and sing-alongs for all.

Cape Cod National Seashore. The 27,700-acre national park includes and protects 30 mi of beaches on the Atlantic coast, as well as woods, swamps, marshland, dunes, and historic structures (including the United States' first transatlantic wireless station and an old lifesaving station). Lacing through the areas are self-guided nature trails and biking and horseback-riding trails. For more information on what the park has to offer, including an extensive program of guided walks, boat trips, and lectures, visit one of the visitor centers off Route 6 (Salt Pond, Eastham, tel. 508/255–3421, closed weekdays Jan.–Feb.; Province Lands, Provincetown, tel. 508/487–1256, closed Dec.–Apr.), which also have nature displays, films, and gift shops. In January and February, information is available at Seashore headquarters, at the Marconi Station (Off Rte. 6, South Wellfleet, tel. 508/349–3785).

Chatham Fish Pier. The unloading of the boats as the fishing fleet returns to the pier on Shore Road in the early afternoon is a big event, drawing crowds that watch from an observation deck.

Cranberry Harvests. Cranberries are big business on the Cape. If you drive along Route 6A in Sandwich in early fall, when the surrounding foliage starts taking on the rich colors, you can watch the cranberries being harvested. First, a bog is flooded with 12 to 18 inches of water, then men in great waders walk a machine with wooden paddles around in it to loosen the berries. Bright red cranberries float on the surface of the water, and more men in waders corral the berries within floating wooden booms, directing the flow into a gathering machine. A conveyor belt deposits them snugly in huge dump trucks.

Heritage Plantation (Grove and Pine Sts., Sandwich, tel. 508/888–3300; closed late-Oct.–mid-May). At this extraordinary 76-acre complex, you'll find extensive gardens—daylily, fruit tree, rhododendron—crisscrossed by walking paths. Also here are museums that showcase classic and historic cars; antique firearms, hand-painted miniature soldiers, and military uniforms; Currier and Ives prints, Americana (such as antique toys and mechanical banks); and a working 1912 carousel. During the summer evening concerts are held on the grounds.

John F. Kennedy Hyannis Museum. While fund-raising continues for a complete museum dedicated to JFK's Cape Cod years, a photographic exhibit is on view at 397 Main Street in Hyannis (tel. 508/790–3077). The photographs, which span the years 1934 to 1963, have been culled largely from the collection of the John Fitzgerald Kennedy Library in Boston.

John F. Kennedy Memorial. The Kennedys have had homes in Hyannis Port, an area of quietly posh estates, since 1929; during John F. Kennedy's presidency, the family compound became the summer White House. This memorial—a quiet esplanade with a plaque and fountain pool overlooking Lewis Bay, on which the late president often sailed—was erected in 1966 by the townspeople. To reach it from Hyannis, take Main Street to Ocean Street.

Lighthouses. Go to *Chatham Light* (Shore Rd.) for a great view of the harbor, the offshore bars, and the ocean beyond. Coin-operated telescopes offer a close look at the famous Chatham Break, where a 1987 storm blasted a channel through a barrier beach. *Highland Light* in Truro (off Rte. 6), the Cape's oldest lighthouse, is where Thoreau boarded for a spell. *Nobska Light* in Woods Hole (Church St.) gives spectacular views of the Elizabeth Islands and Martha's Vineyard.

Monomoy National Wildlife Refuge. This two-island sanctuary off the coast of Chatham is an important stop along the North Atlantic Flyway for migratory waterfowl (peak times are late May and late September), providing resting and nesting grounds for 285 species. White-tailed deer live here, and harbor seals frequent the shores in winter. You can visit this very peaceful place of sand and beach grass, tidal flats and dunes, and an old lighthouse on tours offered by the *Wellfleet Bay Wildlife Sanctuary* (tel. 508/349–2615); you can also get a water taxi at Chatham Harbor (tel. 508/430–2346) to whisk you over in season.

Nickerson State Park. This park (Rte. 6A, Brewster, tel. 508/896–3491 or 508/896–4615 for camping reservations), encompassing more than 1,900 acres of white pine, hemlock, and spruce forest and eight freshwater kettle ponds, offers the Cape's best tent camping; it is also open for fishing (ponds are stocked with trout and bass), biking (8 mi of paved trails), bird-watching, canoeing and sailing, and picnicking; in winter there are ice fishing, skating, and cross-country skiing.

Pilgrim Monument. Dominating the skyline of Provincetown is this 252-ft-high stone tower, erected between 1907 and 1910 to commemorate the landing of the Pilgrims in Provincetown Harbor and the signing of the Mayflower Compact before they moved on to Plymouth. Climb the 116 steps for a panoramic view of the dunes, the harbor, the town, and the entire bay side of Cape Cod. At the base is a museum (tel. 508/487–1310, closed Dec.–Apr.) with exhibits on whaling, shipwrecks, and scrimshaw; a diorama of the *Mayflower;* and more.

Provincetown. A destination in itself, Provincetown (Chamber of Commerce, tel. 508/487–3424) is a quiet fishing village in the winter. During the summer it becomes a lively place, with important art galleries and museums, wonderful crafts shops, whale-watch excursion boats, good restaurants and people-watching, and lots of nightlife (including drag shows). Recently it was designated a historic district, preserving for posterity its cheerful mix of tiny waterfront shops (former fish shacks) and everything from a 1746 Cape house to a Second Empire building. See the town via the *P-town Trolley* (tel. 508/487–9483); see the dunes by Jeep with *Art's Dune Tours* (tel. 508/487–1950).

Sandwich. A picture-perfect New England town, Sandwich is centered by an idyllic pond with shade trees, ducks, children fishing, and a waterwheel-operated gristmill reached by a wooden bridge. You can spend a day wandering in and out of several museums, such as the *Yesteryears Doll Museum* (143 Main St., tel. 508/888–1711; closed Nov.–mid-May), whose collection includes such exotica as lacquer-and-gold miniatures of a Japanese emperor and empress and their court; the *Hoxie House* (18 Water St., tel. 508/888–1173; closed mid-Oct.–mid-June), a furnished and exhibit-filled 1675 saltbox that was never modernized with electricity or plumbing; the *Thornton W. Burgess Museum* (4 Water St., tel. 508/888–4668), dedicated to the native son who created an American Peter Rabbit; and the *Sandwich Glass Museum* (129 Main St., tel. 508/888–0251; closed Jan.), displaying the pressed and blown glass that made the town famous.

Train Tour. *Cape Cod Scenic Railroad* (Main and Center Sts., Hyannis, tel. 508/771–3788 or 800/872-4508 in MA; tours mid-June–Oct.) runs two- and three-hour excursions—past ponds, cranberry bogs, and marshes—between Sagamore and Hyannis, with stops at Sandwich and the canal.

Whale-Watching. Provincetown is the center for whale-watch excursions, which run from spring through fall. On boats of the *Dolphin Fleet* (tel. 508/349–1900 or 800/826–9300), scientists conducting marine research tell you the histories and habits of the mammals. The office (and those of other outfitters) is at MacMillan Wharf, the departure point for the boats. Tours are also available out of Barnstable Harbor (tel. 508/362–6088 or 800/287–0374).

Beaches

All the Atlantic Ocean beaches are cold though otherwise superior—wide, long, sandy, and dune-backed, they usually have lifeguards and rest rooms, but no food. **Coast Guard Beach,** backed by low grass and heathland, and **Nauset Light Beach** are both off Route 6 in Eastham (for Coast Guard, park at the Salt Pond Visitor Center—*see* Cape Cod National Seashore, *above*). In Dennis, off Route 6A, **Corporation Beach** (full services) is a long, broad crescent of white sand; **Chapin Beach** (no services), backed by low dunes, has long tidal flats that allow walking far out at low tide; and sandy-bottomed **Scargo Lake** (rest rooms) is a freshwater lake with a picnic area. **Old Silver Beach** (full services) in North Falmouth, off Route 28, is especially good for small children because a sandbar keeps it shallow at one end and creates tidal pools with crabs and minnows. **Sandy Neck Beach** in West Barnstable is a 6-mi-long barrier beach between bay and marsh, excellent for walking. **West Dennis Beach** (full services) runs 1½ mi along the warm south shore and includes a playground and windsurfing area.

Shopping

Throughout the Cape you'll find shops that sell the fine wares of weavers, glassblowers, potters, and other craftsmen—especially along Route 6A (Old King's Highway), which also has many antiques shops and antiquarian book-sellers. Provincetown was an art colony in the early 1900s and remains an important art center, with many galleries and frequent exhibitions of Cape and non-Cape artists; its crafts offerings are also among the area's most original and sophisticated. Wellfleet has a number of arts and crafts galleries as well all in a quietly artsy setting. Hyannis's Main Street is the Cape's busiest, fun for strolling and people-watching. For buying, head to Provincetown or to Chatham, which has generally traditional antiques and clothing shops and a subdued but charming old-Cape atmosphere. Seven **Christmas Tree Shops** are perennial Cape favorites for a day or night of fun—here you can find discounted paper goods, candles, home furnishings, food, and even clothes. The largest is in Hyannis (Rte. 132, tel. 508/778–5521); the more architecturally interesting shop—complete with whirling windmill and thatched roof—is at exit 1 off Route 6 in Sagamore (tel. 508/888–7010).

Restaurants

At **Regatta of Falmouth-by-the-Sea** (217 Clinton Ave., Falmouth Harbor, tel. 508/548–5400) Continental and Asian cuisines collide, making seafood meals less traditional yet very appealing. The **Beach House** (674 Rte. 6A, Sandwich, tel. 508/362–6403) serves generous portions of seafood, with a rib or two thrown in. **Mattakeese Wharf** (271 Millway, Barnstable Harbor, tel. 508/362–4511), a traditional seaside haunt, has good chowder and a very tasty bouillabaisse.

In Hyannis try the **Roadhouse Café** (488 South St., tel. 508/775–2386), a smart spot that offers a different veal chop special each night as well as gourmet pizza; **Harry's** (700 Main St., tel. 508/778–4188) for Cajun and Creole cuisine; or **Sam Diego's** (950 Iyanough Rd., Rte. 132, tel. 508/771–8816) for Mexican. For a taste of northern Italian cooking try **Abbicci** (43 Main St., Yarmouth, tel. 508/362–3501) or **Gina's by the Sea** (134 Taunton Ave., Dennis, tel. 508/385–3213). The traditional Italian menu at **Christine's** (581 Main St., Rte. 28, West Dennis, tel. 508/394–7333) is made more lively with Middle Eastern touches. At **Vining's Bistro** (595 Main St., Chatham, tel. 508/945–5033) the cuisine is exotic and varied, with such dishes as Bangkok fisherman's stew and spit-roasted Jamaican chicken.

Kadee's Lobster & Clam Bar (Main St., Orleans, tel. 508/255–6184) is a summer seafood landmark that harks back to an era when drive-ins were the norm. **Aesop's Tables** (316 Main St., Wellfleet, tel. 508/349–6450) specializes in seafood entrées and appetizers that take the local Wellfleet oyster to new heights. **Finley JP's** (Rte. 6, South Wellfleet, tel. 508/349–7500) turns out food full of the best Italian influences and ingredients. In Provincetown try **Front Street** (230 Commercial St., tel. 508/487–9715) for Italian; the **Mews** (429 Commercial St., tel. 508/487–1500) or **Bubala's by the Bay** (183 Commercial St., tel. 508/487–0773) for seafood; and **Mojo's** (5 Ryder St. Extension, tel. 508/487–3140) for eclectic fast-food fare (from steak subs and fries to tofu burgers and hummus).

Nightlife and the Arts

In 1916 a young unknown playwright arrived in Provincetown to try his hand at writing plays. In July of that same year, Eugene O'Neill's first play, *Bound East for Cardiff*, made its debut in a waterfront fish house to tremendous success. And so the Provincetown Players prospered. Today, more than 80 years later, theater continues to thrive on Cape Cod. The country's most renowned summer theater, the **Cape Playhouse** (Off Rte. 6A, Dennis, tel. 508/385-3911)—Bette Davis got her start first as an usher, then as an actress, here—tops the list for the best and brightest stage fare. But amateur and community theater abounds as well. Lifting the curtain on the cream of the crop: The **Barnstable Comedy Club** (Village Hall, Rte. 6A, Barnstable, tel. 508/362-6333), the **Academy Playhouse** (120 Main St., Orleans, tel. 508/255-1963), the **Wellfleet Harbor Actors Theater** (Kendrick Ave., Wellfleet, tel. 508/349-6835), and the newest kid on the creative block, the Equity **Provincetown Repertory Theatre** (High Pole Hill Rd., Provincetown, tel. 508/487-0600).

Reservations Services

Bed and Breakfast Cape Cod (Box 341, West Hyannis Port 02672-0341, tel. 508/775-2772 or 800/686-5252), **House Guests Cape Cod and the Islands** (Box 1881, Orleans 02653, tel. 800/666-4678), **Orleans Bed & Breakfast Associates** (Box 1312, Orleans 02653, tel. 508/255-3824 or 800/541-6226; covers Lower Cape, Harwich to Truro), **Provincetown Reservations System** (293 Commercial St., Provincetown 02657, tel. 508/487-2400 or 800/648-0364; also shows, restaurants, and more).

Visitor Information

Cape Cod Chamber of Commerce (Junction of Rtes. 6 and 132, Hyannis 02601, tel. 508/362-3225 or 888/332-2732). **Provincetown Business Guild** (115 Bradford St., Box 421-89, Provincetown 02657, tel. 508/487-2313) focuses on gay tourism.

Ashley Manor

3660 Main St. (Rte. 6A, Box 856), Barnstable 02630, tel. 508/362-8044 or 888/535-2246, fax 508/362-9927

Set off from Old King's Highway by a high privet hedge is this gabled Colonial, built in 1699 with additions tacked on as the years have gone by. The brick patio out back overlooks the inn's 2 quiet acres, complete with a tree-shaded tennis court and a rose-trellised fountain garden.

Inside, the public rooms are large and bright; the living room has a fireplace and Asian rugs. Guest rooms are done in antiques but have such modern comforts as coffeemakers and large baths with hair dryers; all but one have a fireplace. One room has a terrace under the trees, and a separate cottage room (with a whirlpool bath) has sliders out to a deck.

Innkeeper Donald Bain—formerly a New York lawyer—presides over a gourmet breakfast (homemade egg dishes, specialty cereals, fresh fruits, and pastries that have been featured in the pages of *Gourmet* and *Bon Appetite*) served on china either on the terrace or by fire- and candlelight in the formal dining room. (Note that this inn is not suitable for preteens.)

▦ *2 doubles with bath, 3 suites, 1 cottage. Air-conditioning in rooms and suites, minirefrigerator in cottage, bicycles, tennis court, croquet. $120–$180; full breakfast. D, MC, V. No smoking, no pets. 2-night minimum weekends, 3-night minimum holidays.*

Augustus Snow House

528 Main St., Harwich Port 02646, tel. 508/430-0528 or 800/320-0528

This turn-of-the-century Queen Anne Victorian, with gabled dormers and a wraparound veranda, is reminiscent of another era. Throughout, you'll see painstaking attention to period detail in the carefully chosen reproduction and antique furnishings, the dark Victorian-print wallpapers, the rich carpets, and the antique brass bathroom and lighting fixtures. Comfort and luxury abound—from baths with whirlpools to hand-stitched quilts to three-course breakfasts.

Originally from New Jersey, owners Joyce and Steve Roth bought the property in 1996 after an introduction to the B&B business through Joyce's sister, who also runs a guest house. Their love of the beauty and history of the house is obvious; they work hard to maintain that stepped-back-in-time feeling, yet they appreciate your needs for modern comforts. Each of the five rooms is named after (and decorated in honor of) women they hold dear—their three daughters and their mothers. Belle's Room has a summery, country feel and is done in cornflower blue and white. Rose's Room illustrates the shades of her name in Victorian florals.

In the morning a lavish spread is served in the oak-paneled breakfast room. The menu features such delectables as peach kuchen, baked pears in a raspberry cream sauce, and apple-cinnamon quiche. Downstairs, a tea room—decorated to look like a country garden, with old brick walls, stenciled vines and roses, and wrought-iron tables with lace tablecloths—is open to the public Thursday, Friday, and Saturday afternoons. There are also special teatime events once a month.

The elegant parlor off the entrance hall serves as a common area and is a good place to read or mingle with other guests. In cooler weather a welcoming fire blazes in the hearth. In summer you can watch fireflies flicker from the wicker-filled screened-in porch.

▦ *5 doubles with bath. Tea room; air-conditioning; cable TV, phones in rooms; whirlpool tubs in 3 rooms; turndown service. $145–$160; full breakfast. AE, MC, V. No smoking in common areas, no pets. 2-night minimum weekends in peak season.*

Bay Beach

3 Bay Beach La. (Box 151), Sandwich 02563, tel. 508/888–8813 or 800/475–6398

If you're looking for a place where you can step out your sliding glass doors and, in just a minute, dive into the sea, this B&B is calling your name. A mile's walk from Sandwich center via a boardwalk, this modern bay-front house is surrounded on three sides by beach grass.

The decor is contemporary, with lots of light wood, skylights, sand-color carpeting, rattan, pastel fabrics, and brass. The spacious guest rooms have many amenities, including CD/cassette players and radios and bright new baths with hair dryers and heat lamps. Each of the two popular honeymoon suites has a two-person Jacuzzi and mirrored walls behind the beds. (Though couples will like the atmosphere here, families traveling with children may not.)

Emily and Reale Lemieux, innkeepers since 1988, believe in remaining unobtrusive yet always within reach. Breakfast is set out buffet style so you can enjoy it in your room, on your private deck, in the living room, or on the waterfront common deck.

🏠 *3 doubles with bath, 3 suites. Airconditioning, cable TV, phones, minirefrigerators in rooms; complimentary morning newspaper; exercise machines; private beach; beach chairs. $160–$225; Continental-plus breakfast, wine and cheese on arrival. MC, V. No smoking, no pets. 2-night minimum weekends, 3-night minimum holiday weekends. Closed Oct.–mid-May.*

Beach House Inn

61 Uncle Stephen's Way (Box 494), West Dennis 02670, tel. 508/398–4575 or 617/489–4144 off-season

If the Beach House Inn were any closer to the water, you'd be sleeping with the fish. Here Nantucket Sound is your backyard: Shingles are weathered gray from salt air; you're surrounded by white wicker and natural oak furniture that's practical yet comfortable; and walls of glass frame the beauty—and, sometimes, the ferocity—of the Cape.

There are seven rooms on two floors, and all have decks and are decorated in the same plain maple and wicker flavors (but let's face it—you probably didn't come here for the furniture). Some rooms have brass or four-poster beds, ceiling fans, and views of the front yard. Room 2 has a second-story deck with a staircase down to the private beach.

The common room has a TV and wide assortment of hit movies on video. You can use the barbecue grills or the fully equipped kitchen—if that fresh cup of coffee doesn't wake you up, then the sight of the crashing waves just beyond the sliding glass doors certainly will. There's also a private, fenced-in playground for when the young (and young-at-heart) no longer want to frolic in the water or build sand castles.

🏠 *7 doubles with bath. TVs in all rooms, ceiling fans in some rooms, private beach, playground, shuffleboard. $75–$105; Continental-plus breakfast. No credit cards. No smoking, no pets. 2-night minimum weekends and holidays in peak season.*

Beechwood Inn

2839 Main St. (Rte. 6A), Barnstable 02630, tel. 508/362–6618 or 800/609–6618, fax 508/362–0298

This 1853 Queen Anne Victorian, painted yellow and pale green and trimmed with gingerbread, is on tree-lined Old King's Highway. Wrapping it on three sides is a porch where wicker chairs and rockers sit beneath wind chimes in the shade of an ancient weeping beech.

Hosts Debbie and Ken Traugot have maintained the Victorian theme inside. In the parlor mahogany and red velvet furnishings blend with Victorian-patterned wallpaper. In a cozy adjacent room—with wainscoting, a pressed-tin ceiling, and a fireplace—breakfast is served at tables covered in lace and set with hurricane lamps, flowers, china, and crystal. (Families should note that such touches make this inn unsuitable for curious youngsters; teenagers will be comfortable here, though.)

Guest rooms are done in a lighter, early Victorian style and have pedestal sinks, antique plumbing and lighting fixtures, wicker pieces, Asian rugs, and lacy curtains. The decor in the popular, romantic Rose Room is a little heavier with a working fireplace; a high, queen-size mahogany four-poster bed with a crocheted canopy and spread; and a red velvet fainting couch.

🏨 *6 doubles with bath. Air-conditioning in 3 rooms, minirefrigerators, bicycles, volleyball, badminton. $130–$150; full breakfast, afternoon tea. AE, MC, V. No smoking, no pets. 2-night minimum weekends in peak season, 3-night minimum holidays.*

The Brass Key

9 Court St., Provincetown 02657, tel. 508/ 487–9005 or 800/842–9858, fax 508/487– 9020

On a quiet side street just a block from the center of town, this 1828 sea captain's home is fast becoming a premier guest house. The entire property has been completely and luxuriously restored, and it now includes several buildings as well as the original house.

Owner Michael MacIntyre, a Ritz-Carlton alum, and his partner, Bob Anderson, have balanced modern convenience with rustic charm. The rooms are cozy and have exquisitely papered and/or stenciled interiors and wall-to-wall carpeting. They're furnished with simple country-style antiques such as pencil-post, sleigh, and canopy beds; carved wood armoires; and slant-top writing desks. One of the

more spacious rooms is done in rich hues of burgundy and gold and has a queen-size bed with a headboard made from a fireplace mantel. Amenities here go beyond the usual creature comforts: Bose stereos, Caswell & Massey toiletries, hair dryers, and bathrobes. Deluxe rooms have gas fireplaces, whirlpool tubs, and private decks. Two rooms are cottages in an enclosed brick courtyard.

A heated outdoor pool provides a freshwater alternative to the beach. Little umbrella tables are set about for those who prefer the shade. There are also common decks, including a widow's walk roof deck with spectacular views of Cape Cod bay. In season complimentary Cape Codders (vodka and cranberry juice) are served in the courtyard beside the huge, hot-spa dip pool. In winter wine is served beside a roaring fire in the sitting-dining area, which has wide-board floors, original beams and wainscoting, and a beautiful antique table that was once used for kneading dough. Each morning one can help yourself at a buffet.

The Brass Key attracts a large gay clientele, especially in summer. The attentive staff makes everyone welcome and comfortable and offers tips about not-to-be-missed events in town.

🏨 *34 doubles with bath. Air-conditioning, cable TV/VCRs, phones, minirefrigerators, hair dryers, bathrobes in rooms; video library; turndown service; heated spa pool; heated outdoor pool. $185–$335; Continental breakfast. AE, MC, V. No smoking in common and some guest rooms, no pets. Minimum stay required in season, on holidays, and during special events (number of nights varies).*

Brewster Farmhouse

716 Main St., Brewster 02631, tel. 508/ 896–3910 or 800/892–3910, fax 508/896– 4232

This 1850 farmhouse blends gently with its surroundings across from a 19th-century windmill on historic Route 6A. Through its portals, however, some lovely 20th-century surprises await. Sliding glass doors lead from a common area with a fireplace to a patio with café tables. Beyond, the backyard has a pool and spa and is rimmed with apple trees and grapevines.

Carol and Gary Concors bought the inn in 1996 with one goal in mind: create a casual yet elegant haven. The sophisticated guest rooms have antiques and Lane reproduction furnishings, large modern baths, quilts, goose-down pillows, terry robes, hair dryers, and sherry and chocolates by the bed. The large downstairs guest rooms include one with a fireplace; one with a king-size bed and a private patio; and a third with a mammoth, acorn-carved, queen-size four-poster. Each morning, Gary, an award-winning pastry chef, concocts a full country breakfast, which is served on a long wooden table in the dining area.

▦ *3 doubles with bath, 1 suite. Air-conditioning, cable TV in rooms, turndown service, heated pool/spa, beach towels and blankets, bicycles. $110–$175; full breakfast and afternoon tea. AE, D, DC, MC, V. No smoking, no pets.*

The Captain Farris House

308 Old Main St., South Yarmouth 02664, tel. 508/760–2818 or 800/350–9477, fax 508/398–1262

Steps from the Bass River Bridge, which divides South Yarmouth and West Dennis, and a short way from congested Route 28 sits this 1845 Greek Revival home that was built by the sea captain for whom it is named. In 1996 innkeepers Stephen and Patty Bronstein took over the newly refurbished and restored home, turning it into a first-class B&B—enriching its look while maintaining its hold on the past.

Your eye cannot possibly take it all in at once: Tasteful reproductions of priceless artwork hang everywhere, and nooks and crannies are crammed with collectibles, coveted treasures, and sculptures. The French salon–style living room has a 1920s baby grand that you can play if you're so inclined. The dining room walls are painted to look as if they're covered with wallpaper, and the room has art and antiques that would be the envy of even the most jaded collector (the many antiques make this inn inappropriate for children). And don't forget to investigate the unique dining table . . . can you figure out its secret?

Guest rooms are large and comfortable with antique or canopy beds; extra pillows; plush comforters; and tiled sunken baths that have a Jacuzzi, a hair dryer, and imported toiletries. Two have fireplaces and sundecks. The Honeymoon Suite has both a sundeck and a two-person Jacuzzi. In each room fancy drapes fill the windows; fancier antiques and quality reproductions fill the rest of the space.

Breakfast is served in the dining room or in the brick courtyard—a slice of Tuscany right on the Mid-Cape.

▦ *8 doubles with bath, 4 suites. Air-conditioning in 3 rooms; TVs, phones, Jacuzzis, hair dryers in all rooms. $95–$185; full breakfast. AC, MC, V. No smoking, no pets. 2-night minimum weekends, 3-night minimum holidays.*

Captain Freeman Inn

15 Breakwater Rd., Brewster 02631, tel. 508/896–7481 or 800/843–4664

This impressive Victorian faces Brewster's little town square and was built in 1866 by a packet-schooner captain and fleet owner. Converted to an inn in the 1940s, it was bought in December 1991 by Carol Covitz, a former marketing director for a Boston computer company.

Carol has restored the exterior's original Victorian greens and used contrasting colors for the brackets and columns of the wraparound veranda. The veranda itself got a new floor of oiled mahogany and has rockers and a screened section facing the pool. Inside, the ground floor rooms have 12-ft ceilings and windows and such fine details as ornate Italian-plaster ceiling medallions and a marble fireplace brought back from the captain's travels.

Guest rooms have hardwood floors, local art, antiques and Victorian reproductions, crystal or brass lamps, eyelet spreads, and all-cotton sheets; most beds have lace or fishnet canopies. Like the common areas, first-floor rooms have 12-ft ceilings, grand windows, and ceiling medallions. Second- and third-floor front rooms offer 8½-ft ceilings and large windows with views of a white steepled church and the square. In a 1989 addition there are three spacious bedrooms with queen-size canopy beds, sofas, fireplaces, cable TV and VCRs, minirefrigerators, and French doors that lead to enclosed porches with whirlpool spas.

Carol's breakfasts showcase skills honed in professional cooking classes. (In winter she runs her own cooking school on weekends.) Such dishes as potato-cheddar pie, Italian *stradas*, and compotes are served on the screened porch or by the fire in the dining room.

Out back, the 1½-acre lawn is bordered in wild grapes, blackberries, and high-bush blueberries. Hurricane fencing surrounds the pool and its deck, which is edged by garden and set with lounge chairs. A bay beach is a five-minute walk away.

🏨 *9 doubles with bath, 3 doubles share bath. Common refrigerator and ice maker; minirefrigerators in some rooms; movie library; outdoor heated pool; croquet; badminton; bicycles. $95–$135, suites $225; full breakfast, afternoon tea. AE, MC, V. No smoking, no pets. 2-night minimum in peak season and on weekends.*

Captain's House Inn

371 Old Harbor Rd., Chatham 02633, tel. 508/945-0127, fax 508/945-0866

Finely preserved architectural details, superb decor, luscious baked goods, and a feeling of warmth make this a fine inn, indeed. The complex is on 2 acres—behind a high hedge—about ½ mi from town center. It consists of the main inn, a white Greek Revival built in 1839 by packet-boat captain Hiram Harding; the attached carriage house, a three-quarter Cape; the Captain's Cottage, a full Cape (with a 200-year-old bow roof) in its own yard with a lovely English garden; and the recently renovated Stables, a separate building with three suites.

Though the general style of the inn is Williamsburg—with historic-reproduction wallpapers, mostly king- and queen-size canopy or other antique beds, and upholstered wing chairs—each guest room has its own personality. Wild Pigeon is spacious and serene, with an antique canopied four-poster and cream Berber wall-to-wall carpeting under a high cathedral ceiling. In the Captain's Cottage, the Hiram Harding Room has 200-year-old hand-hewn beams, a wall of Early American raised walnut paneling, a large fireplace flanked by wing chairs, a sofa in front of wall-to-wall shelves holding antique books, and a rich red Asian carpet. The luxury suites in the Stables have every amenity, including remote-control gas fireplaces, separate "spas" with double whirlpool tubs, balconies, TV/VCRs, refrigerators, and coffeemakers.

In the main inn the entry hall's pumpkin-pine floors shine softly. Here and in the parlor, where a hearth fire welcomes you on chilly days, impeccably chosen antiques are accompanied by luxurious Oriental carpets and oil paintings of sea captains. French doors lead to a sunroom, where breakfast and a lavish English tea (with homemade scones, jams, and cream) are served on Wedgwood and crystal at individual tables.

Jan and Dave McMaster spent nearly two years in search of their perfect inn and became owners of the Captain's House in June 1993. Dave, a retired Navy commander and ex-CEO of a computer company, and Jan, a gracious English-woman with a knack of making you feel special, run the inn with a well-trained staff that includes English university students studying hotel management and catering. A full gourmet breakfast is served, and there are honeymoon baskets, courtesy bicycles, and lawn croquet in the warmer months.

🏨 *14 doubles with bath, 5 suites. Air-conditioning in all rooms; TVs/VCRs, refrigerators, coffeemakers, whirlpool baths in some rooms; croquet; bicycles. $135–$325; full breakfast, afternoon tea. AE, MC, V. No smoking, no pets.*

Chatham Bars Inn

Shore Rd., Chatham 02633, tel. 508/945–0096 or 800/527–4884, fax 508/945–5491

Atop a rise that overlooks Pleasant Bay, just a stroll from the shops of Chatham, is this old-style oceanfront resort. Built as a hunting lodge in 1914 and once used as an exclusive club, Chatham Bars remains a classy place. The crescent-shape main building and 26 one- to eight-bedroom cottages (either in woods near the main inn or across the street on the bluff above the beach) are set on 20 landscaped acres. You're surrounded by elegance here, so feel free to dress in your best during peak season (no jeans or T-shirts in common areas after 6 PM).

Most rooms have decks, and all the cottages have common rooms, some with fireplaces. Throughout, rooms are carpeted in shades of sand and sea and are attractively appointed with traditional pine pieces, more modern upholstered pieces, Queen Anne reproductions, gilt-framed art, and Laura Ashley touches.

Off the grand entry hall is the South Lounge, which has Victorian-style overstuffed chairs and comfortable couches

in burgundy and beige, pots of eucalyptus, and an enormous fireplace; a brick terrace with views of the bay and the famous sandbars; and a year-round casual restaurant-bar. The elegant main dining room has a wall of windows with sea views and a crisp decor with a deep green rug offset by white accents. The lavish breakfast buffet is served here and includes fresh fruits, sliced meats, smoked fish, and finger pastries; hot dishes are also available. At dinner expect creative takes on traditional New England fare. The beach house grill has lighter meals and clambakes in summer, and the tavern offers upscale pub grub year-round.

🏨 *136 doubles with bath, 22 suites. 3 restaurants; phones, cable TV in rooms; cottages with common minirefrigerators; lending library; movies; exercise room; cocktail parties; children's program (July–Aug.); complimentary newspapers; baby-sitting services; private beach; 4 tennis courts; putting green; heated outdoor pool; volleyball; harbor cruises; launch service. $170–$1,000; breakfast extra. AE, DC, MC, V. No pets.*

The Four Chimneys Inn

946 Main St. (Rte. 6A), Dennis 02638, tel. 508/385–6317 or 800/874–5502, fax 508/385–6285

Under the careful (and highly creative) guidance of congenial Russell and Kathy Tomasetti, this three-story, four-chimney, 1881 Queen Anne Victorian, once home to the town doctor, has been transformed into a relaxing getaway (leave the wee ones at home). The eight guest rooms, whose doors bear embroidered signs displaying their names—TEABERRY and BLUEBERRY, for example—vary in size and decor, but all are tastefully done with cherry four-poster, wicker, or antique pine or oak beds; quilts; and hand-stenciled trim. Three rooms have decorative fireplaces, and all have views of either Scargo Lake or the surrounding woods and flowering gardens. The Berry

Patch Room is intimate (read: small) but charming, with original wide-plank floors, wicker galore, and stained-glass window details. For seclusion book the second-floor Strawberry Suite, which has a sitting area and a bedroom so large that there's room for queen- and twin-size beds. The suite's deck overlooks rolling lawns and gardens.

Most guests opt to enjoy Kathy's hearty breakfasts in the high-ceilinged dining room (where they can also admire the cranberry glass collection), but the screened-in summer porch, with its lovely garden views, is a more soothing spot. After a day of relaxing—or recreation—nothing could be finer than sitting under the wisteria-draped arbor and sipping afternoon tea.

▦ *7 doubles with bath, 1 suite. Ceiling fans, TVs in 6 rooms and common room. $85–$125; Continental-plus breakfast. AE, D, MC, V. Restricted smoking, no pets. 2-night minimum weekends, 3-night minimum holidays. Closed late Oct.–late Apr.*

Heaven on High

70 High St., West Barnstable 02668, tel. 508/362–4441 or 800/362–4044, fax 508/362–4465

This 11-year-old B&B is, indeed, heaven, nestled as it is high on a hill—and on one of the Cape's oldest roads—overlooking dunes, the Great Salt Marsh, and the Bay at Sandy Neck. Opened in 1996 by displaced Connecticutites Deanna and Gib Katten, it is a feast for the spirit. The fantasy begins before you step inside: Deanna is an award-winning horticulturist, and the grounds demonstrate her talents. The garden motif spills into the house. The walls of the main foyer are a jungle of hand-stenciled and hand-painted sunflowers, ivy, and hummingbirds. (Look up: The ceilings have billowing clouds.)

Throughout, the decor is a mixture of California beach house and Cape Cod comfort—light, airy, and breezy. Deanna is also a collector; you'll find her treasures—one-of-a-kind miniature dressers, autographs (Al Jolson, Eleanor Roosevelt, Groucho Marx), priceless Tiffany silver—grouped here, there, and everywhere (such bits and bobs make this inn unsuitable for children). The Great Room has overstuffed chairs and couches, a fireplace, a TV, natural oak flooring, and a classical CD collection. Sliding glass doors lead to a peaceful living room and a deck that runs the length of the house. From here you have unobstructed views of sand and surf.

Three immense, immaculate guest rooms are filled with enviable antiques, walk-in closets, and unsurpassed decorative details (each room is named for the collection that it houses). The luxurious Silhouettes and Mirrors Room extends the width of the house and is fully carpeted. It has a queen-size bed, a fireplace, a tiled bath with two vanity sinks, a large deck, and, of course, silhouettes and mirrors of all types. Each room has a vintage handkerchief collection, and you are encouraged to take one as a memento. There's also an extensive audiobook collection for the long trip home; Deanna and Gib trust you to send the tapes back.

At breakfast the table is set with fine china and Tiffany silverware (Deanna smiles when she boasts that she can set the table for a whole month and not duplicate a place setting). The food is just as fine, featuring such culinary concoctions as tiramisu French toast, pear pancakes, and pineapple-walnut-raisin muffins—just one more reason to try to get to Heaven.

▦ *3 doubles with bath. Air-conditioning, minirefrigerators in rooms; TV in living room. $110–$130; full breakfast. No smoking, no pets. MC, V. 2-night minimum weekends, 3-night minimum holidays in peak season.*

The Inn at Fernbrook

481 Main St., Centerville 02632, tel. 508/ 775–4334, fax 508/778–4455

When Boston restaurateur Howard Marston built this Queen Anne–style mansion in quiet Centerville, just outside Hyannis, he hired the best—Frederick Law Olmsted, designer of New York's Central Park—to landscape it. In Marston's day there were 17 acres of man-made ponds, formal gardens, a vineyard, and hundreds of trees brought from all over the world by Marstons's sea captain father. Though the estate has dwindled to 2 acres, the fern-rimmed brook and part of Olmsted's design remain. Pebbled paths wind past a sunken sweetheart garden of red and pink roses set in a heart-shape lawn, exotic trees (a Japanese cork, a weeping beech), a windmill, a vine-covered arbor, and two ponds where goldfish swim amid water hyacinths and lilies. (Families take note: small children will not be comfortable here, though teenagers probably will.)

The 1881 house itself, now on the National Register of Historic Places, is a beauty—from the turreted white exterior to the fine woodwork and furnishings within. Guest rooms have antique or reproduction beds, 1930s-style wooden table radios, and decanters of sherry with antique glasses. Some have sitting areas with bay windows; fireplaces; Victorian sofas; and pastel Asian carpets on floors of cherry, maple, or oak. The third-floor Olmsted Suite has a sundeck as well as two bedrooms and a living room with a fireplace under cathedral ceilings. There is also a cottage by itself across the lawns.

Although breakfast is served in a formal dining room, the tone of the meal is friendly, and the food is delicious. Brian Gallo—who left the hotel business in 1986 to join his friend Sal Di Florio, who was converting this house into an inn—cooks the meals, and Sal serves. Brian likes to tell of how onetime owner Herbert Kalmus, inventor of the Technicolor process, hosted such Hollywood friends as Gloria Swanson and Cecil B. DeMille and of how Cardinal Spellman (who once used the house as a summer retreat) entertained John F. Kennedy and Richard Nixon. In the afternoon iced or hot tea can be taken (on request) in the living room or on the veranda, with its wicker furniture and hanging flower baskets.

🏨 *5 doubles with bath, 1 suite, 1 cottage. Massage service. $135–$195; full breakfast. AE, D, MC, V. No smoking, no pets. 2-night minimum summer weekends, 3-night minimum holidays in peak season.*

Inn at Sandwich Center

118 Tupper Rd., Sandwich 02563, tel. 508/888–6958 or 800/249–6949

If you want to be spoiled rotten, head straight for the Inn at Sandwich Center. Owner Eliane Thomas will do everything necessary to achieve this goal, which is why so much of her clientele is repeat business. Eliane and her husband, Al, took over the Inn in 1995, after moving to Sandwich from Newport Beach, California. In their hands the 18th-century saltbox (no one knows its exact year, though the handmade brick chimney is dated 1750) has become what French-born Eliane calls "a French country inn with an English accent and an American sense of humor." The house, directly across from the Sandwich Glass Museum, is listed on the National Register of Historic Places.

By candlelight Eliane serves such breakfast specialties as rhubarb muffins or crepes with raspberry sauce in the antiques-furnished keeping room that's replete with fireplace and original 1750 beehive oven. Off the dining room is the common living area that's anything but common: chock-full of art and antiquities accumulated by the Thomases on their worldwide jaunts, it's the perfect place in which to enjoy sherry at the end of a long day. (Children will not appreciate the adult atmosphere here; best to leave them at home.)

Guest rooms have Laura Ashley comforters and bedding, hooked rugs, and such amenities as terry-cloth robes (expect handmade chocolates on your pillow at night, too); three rooms have fireplaces. The Blue Room has a two-poster bed, comfortable rockers, a chintz chaise, and built-in cabinets stuffed full of travel books—great material to peruse on the private deck that overlooks the gardens.

🏨 *5 doubles with bath. Terry-cloth robes in rooms. $85–$110; Continental-plus breakfast. AE, D, MC, V. No smoking, no pets. 2-night minimum weekends and holidays.*

Inn on the Sound

313 Grand Ave., Falmouth Heights 02540, tel. 508/457-9666 or 800/564-9668, fax 508/457-9631

Despite being smack dab on busy Grand Avenue, this inn is very tranquil. You see, it's also on a bluff that overlooks Vineyard Sound and offers glimpses of the island itself. All the rooms, from the living room—with its enormous boulder fireplace, oversized windows, and overstuffed chairs—to each of the 10 guest rooms (all named for various Falmouth area landmarks) face the water.

David Ross owns the inn with his sister, Renee, an interior decorator who knows her stuff. (The atmosphere here is perfect for couples or families with teenagers; this inn is not suitable for small children.) Nobska Light, the only guest room with a fireplace, has a minimalist white-on-white color scheme that plays brilliantly off the sweeping views of the sound. Every room has a queen-size bed and simple, contemporary furnishings: natural oak tables, unbleached cottons, and ceiling fans—the latter really unnecessary owing to the sea breezes.

Common areas include an art-filled living room, a bistrolike breakfast room (try the French toast stuffed with cream cheese), and a 40-ft deck. Go ahead and dawdle.

🏨 *10 doubles with bath. TV in room on request, beach access, beach chairs and towels. $95–$155; full breakfast. AE, D, MC, V. No smoking, no pets. 2-night minimum weekends, 3-night minimum holidays.*

Isaiah Clark House

1187 Rte. 6A (Box 169), Brewster 02631, tel. 508/896-2223 or 800/822-4001, fax 508/896-2138

This three-quarter cape with Colonial-style decor retains the flavor of its 1780 origins with painted floorboards of varying widths, old fireplace mantels and moldings, narrow staircases, and the original keeping room. Some rooms have queen-size canopy beds, wood-burning fireplaces, and Asian rugs; one has a bed beneath a skylight.

For breakfast innkeeper Richard Griffin whips up such delights as cranberry pancakes with three-berry butter. You'll dine in the keeping room or on the sunny deck that overlooks 5 acres of woods, gardens, and a pond—all adjacent to a nature preserve.

🏨 *7 doubles with bath. Air-conditioning; cable TV in rooms; turndown service; games; beach chairs and towels; airport or train-station pickup. $98–$125; full breakfast, afternoon tea, evening cookies and milk on request. AE, D, MC, V. No smoking, no pets. 2-night minimum weekends in peak season.*

Isaiah Hall B&B Inn

152 Whig St. (Box 1007), Dennis 02638, tel. 508/385-9928 or 800/736-0160, fax 508/385-5879

Lilacs and pink roses trail along the white picket fence outside this 1857 Greek Revival farmhouse. Inside, the cheerful, unfussy decor features country antiques, some canopy beds, floral-print wallpapers, and such homey touches as quilts and Priscilla curtains.

In the main house's Early American common room, a coal-burning stove is set inside the fireplace of the original kitchen, complete with beehive oven and a proofing cabinet. In the attached carriage house, rooms have a Cape Cod, cottagelike look, with three stenciled white walls and one wall in knotty pine; several have small balconies overlooking a wooded lawn with grape arbors, berry bushes, and gardens. The Great Room has a TV, white wicker furniture, and an 1857 potbelly stove.

Innkeeper Marie Brophy has provided such thoughtful extras as radio alarm clocks, ironing boards, full-length mirrors, and robes in every room. Make-it-yourself popcorn, tea and coffee, and soft drinks are always available. (Note that teenagers will be comfortable here, but small children will not.)

▥ *9 doubles with bath, 1 suite. Air-conditioning in rooms, minirefrigerator in suite, badminton, croquet. $85–$142; Continental-plus breakfast. AE, MC, V. No smoking, no pets. 3-night minimum weekends and holidays. Closed mid-Oct.–mid-Apr.*

Isaiah Jones Homestead

165 Main St., Sandwich 02563, tel. 508/ 888–9115 or 800/526–1625, fax 508/888– 9648

Built in 1849, everything in this inn reflects the early Victorian era—from the fine antiques, Asian carpets, and elegant window treatments to such period accents as fringed lamp shades, leather-bound books, and a beaded bag on a dresser. Innkeepers Doug and Jan Klapper, who acquired the inn in 1997, serve a homemade, multicourse hot breakfast by candlelight, the gathering room has a fireplace, and you'll find a TV and a minirefrigerator in the study.

The two first-floor rooms have 11-ft ceilings and knockout antique-reproduction beds, including a massive Empire four-poster with a fishnet canopy and a high mahogany bed with pineapple finials on posts encrusted with leaf carvings. Up the curving staircase is the sweet Lombard Jones Room, with maroon damask bedding and a corona canopy and a bath with whirlpool tub. The Deming Jarves Room, the pièce de résistance, has seafoam green wallpaper, an Asian rug, and a stunning suite of burled birch, including a settee, an armoire, and a cheval mirror. The mauve-tile bath has a whirlpool tub. (Note that this inn is not suitable for young children.)

▥ *5 doubles with bath. $95–$155; full breakfast, afternoon tea. AE, D, MC, V. No smoking, no pets. 2-night minimum weekends and holidays.*

Moses Nickerson House

364 Old Harbor Rd., Chatham 02633, tel. 508/945–5859 or 800/628–6972, fax 508/ 945–7087

Linda and George Watts are proof of the magical romantic influence of the Moses Nickerson House. When the company Linda worked for moved its operations to New York City in 1995, Linda quit the corporate world and came back to her roots on the Cape. She'd enjoyed managing a B&B in college, and when she came across this 1839 former whaling captain's home—a white Greek Revival with gray-blue shutters and a large fan ornament—she bought the place. The inn had only been open for a week or so when George drove in from Canada late one afternoon looking for a place to stay. The rest is history. They were married that Thanksgiving and have run the inn together ever since.

Fine antiques, attention to detail, and warm hospitality are the hallmarks here. Breakfast is served on gleaming crystal in the glass sunroom, which has garden views, or in the formal dining room when the weather turns cold. Linda prepares delectable dishes such as egg and cheese casseroles or fruit pizza (a pastry crust topped with cream cheese and a variety of fruit). In the afternoon homemade lemonade is served in the parlor. Here you'll find a fireplace, an Aubusson rug, a lyre-base Duncan Phyfe table, Cape Cod cranberry glass, and a hand-carved Mexican horse inlaid with agates.

Guest rooms have wide-board pine floors and firm queen-size beds with comforters, color-coordinated linens, and lots of pillows; most rooms have pedestal sinks, and several have gas-log fireplaces. Special touches include stenciling, scented drawer liners, padded clothes hangers, and dimmer switches on reading lamps.

Room 7 is clubby and masculine, with Ralph Lauren fabrics, dark leathers and woods, and a fireplace; on the walls hang hunting hats and horns. In Room 4 you need a stool to climb into the canopy bed; a wooden rack displays antique laces and linens, and a Nantucket hand-hooked rug complements the stenciled and whitewashed walls. Off the parlor is Room 1, with a romantic antique four-poster bed and armoire that are hand-painted with roses and a blue velvet Belgian settee before the fireplace.

🏠 *7 doubles with bath. Turndown service in season. $129–$169; full breakfast, afternoon lemonade. AE, MC, V. No smoking, no pets. 2-night minimum summer weekends, 3-night minimum holidays.*

Mostly Hall

27 Main St., Falmouth 02540, tel. 508/ 548-3786 or 800/682-0565

Set behind a high wrought-iron fence, Mostly Hall looks very much like a private estate. Built in 1849 by a sea captain for his New Orleans bride, the gray-clapboard structure has a porch that wraps around the entire first floor and a dramatic cupola. Named for its large central hallways (which, despite

their size, are not places for children to run through; best to leave youngsters at home), the inn offers corner rooms with leafy views, shuttered casement windows, reproduction queen-size canopy beds, floral wallpapers, and wall-to-wall carpeting. Ground-floor rooms have 13-ft ceilings. Most baths are small.

Jim and Caroline Lloyd, innkeepers since 1986, are warm and helpful. Jim's love of clocks is reflected in the eclectic Victorian sitting room, where an 1890 Paris mantel clock and four others chime the hour. Caroline shines at breakfast with such treats as French toast stuffed with cream cheese and walnuts. The inn is just steps from the shops of Falmouth and a few miles from Woods Hole and the Vineyard ferry.

🏠 *6 doubles with bath. Air-conditioning, bicycles. $125; full breakfast, afternoon tea. AE, D, MC, V. No smoking, no pets. 2-night minimum weekends and holidays. Closed Jan.*

Penny House Inn

4885 County Rd. (Rte. 6), North Eastham 02651, tel. 508/255-6632 or 800/554-1751, fax 508/255-4893

Tucked behind a wave of privet hedge, this rambling gray-shingled inn consists of the original 1690 sea captain's home and an early 1980s addition. Most of the rooms are spacious, and they're furnished with a combination of antiques, collectibles, and wicker. Deluxe rooms have air-conditioning, minirefrigerators, and phones. Captain's Quarters has a sitting area in front of a wood-burning fireplace, a king-size brass bed, a miniature library, and a lovely garden view.

Innkeeper Margaret Keith moved to the Cape from Australia in 1988; an antique boomerang and diggerdoo hang over the fireplace mantle. Fond of entertaining, she joins her guests for afternoon tea in the winter and lemonade and cookies on the patio in warmer months.

Common areas include the Great Room, which has a fireplace and lots of windows; the sunroom-library; and the garden patio, which has tables shaded by an umbrella. A full country breakfast, which might include eggs Benedict or pecan waffles with fresh kiwi, is served in the formal dining room at individual tables.

🏨 *11 doubles with bath. Air-conditioning, phones, minirefrigerators in some rooms; TV in common room. $115–$180; full breakfast, afternoon tea. AE, D, MC, V. No smoking, no pets.*

The Ruddy Turnstone

463 Rte. 6A, Brewster 02631, tel. 508/385–9871 or 800/654–1995

Set at the edge of a lawn that gently slopes to a marsh and named for the sea bird that frequents the shore, the Ruddy Turnstone captures the flavor of old New England. Built in the early 1800s and impeccably restored, both the main house and the Nantucket Carriage House have such original architectural details as pine-board floors and numbered-to-fit barn boards.

After spending eight years in New Hampshire as restaurateurs, innkeepers Sally and Gordon Swanson moved back to the Cape in 1992 and turned their considerable energies toward transforming a tumbledown summer home into a first-rate inn. The warm, personable Swansons used their exquisite taste to create surroundings that are both elegant and comfortable.

Rooms in the main house and the Carriage House are furnished with country antiques, braided and Asian rugs, quilts, and queen-size four-poster beds; all have air-conditioning. Baths are large, and most have shower-tub combos. The main house's Bayview Suite has a sitting area in front of a wood-burning fireplace, an acorn-post queen-size bed, and a spectacular view of the ocean—on a clear day you can see the Pilgrim Monument in

Provincetown. Don't despair if this suite is booked—an upstairs common sitting room also offers an incredible view of the marsh and the bay beyond; binoculars are available for bird-watching.

Downstairs a cozy parlor has a TV, a fireplace, and a small library. In the backyard you can relax in hammocks and lounge chairs or play croquet, badminton, or horseshoes. The inn is close to beaches, shops, restaurants, theaters, and galleries.

As you might expect, given the Swansons' restaurant background, breakfast is a real treat. Gordon, a former chef, creates such delectable dishes as baked-apple French toast and scrambled eggs in puff pastry. Breakfast is served at little tables on the porch, which has marsh views, or in the dining room.

🏨 *5 doubles with bath. Guest refrigerator, TV in parlor, croquet, badminton, horseshoes. $95–$150; full breakfast. No smoking. MC, V. Closed Jan.–Feb.*

South Hollow Vineyards Inn

Rte. 6A (Shore Rd., Box 165), North Truro 02652, tel. 508/487–6200, fax 508/487–4248

When innkeepers Judy Wimer and Kathy Gregrow, both with plant science backgrounds, bought the historic Hughes-Rich farmstead, they had a grand plan: transform one of the Cape's last working farms, on 5 rolling acres, into a vineyard. Once they had established the French *vinefera* vines, they then concentrated on turning the run-down 1836 Federal-style house into a romantic guest house.

The vineyard theme continues inside, with a decor of deep greens and burgundies and antique casks and presses tucked into corners. Rooms are elegant and have names relating to the vineyard. All have country antiques, rich carpets, four-poster king- or queen-size beds, and modern tiled baths (most with tub and shower). The Vintage Suite has exposed beams and period furnishings, a king-size four-poster bed, and a large bath with a two-person Jacuzzi.

A full breakfast, often garnished with garden-grown berries, is served in the sunroom or on the patio. A large common sundeck offers a sweeping view of the vineyard and is a perfect place to relax with a book.

🏠 *5 doubles with bath. $89–$129. No smoking. MC, V.*

Village Green Inn

40 Main St., Falmouth 02540, tel. 508/548–5621 or 800/237–1119, fax 508/457–5051

This turreted white Victorian (actually built in 1804 and Victorianized in 1894) across from the Falmouth Green was taken over in 1995 by Don and Dianne Crosby. They've worked hard to preserve such details as the fine old woodwork and hardwood floors (one with inlay from 1890), an elaborately designed forced-hot-water radiator, the stained-glass above the front room picture window, and the embossed-tin ceiling and half wall (the other half is raised oak paneling) in one bath. To this they've added tasteful furnishings and modern comforts. In the spacious guest rooms, two of which have working fireplaces, you'll find antique and reproduction queen-size beds, comforters, dust ruffles, and floral-print wallpapers in soft Victorian colors. (Preteens will not appreciate the atmosphere here; leave your youngest children at home.)

Breakfast features hot entrées like apple-filled German pancakes or chili-cheese egg puffs. Seasonal beverages, such as sherry, hot cider, or lemonade, are served on the veranda, with its wicker and its hanging geraniums, or in the elegant guest parlor, which has a Victorian fireplace.

🏠 *4 doubles with bath, 1 suite. Air-conditioning, cable TV, bicycles. $85–$145; full breakfast. AE, MC, V. No smoking, no pets. 2-night minimum weekends, 3-night minimum holidays.*

Wedgewood Inn

83 Main St., Yarmouth Port 02675, tel. 508/362–5157 or 508/362–9178, fax 508/362–5851

This inn, a handsome 1812 Greek Revival building, is on the National Register of Historic Places. The facade is white with black shutters, the front door has sidelights and a fanlight, and there's a large fan ornament over a third-floor window. Inside, the elegance continues with a sophisticated mix of fine Colonial antiques, hand-crafted cherry pencil-post beds, upholstered wing chairs, Asian rugs on wide-board floors, English sporting prints and maritime paintings, brass accents, antique quilts, Claire Murray hooked rugs, period wallpapers, and wood-burning fireplaces. Five spacious suites (three are in the detached barn, renovated in 1997) have canopy beds, fireplaces, and porches; one has a separate den with a sofa bed and a bay window. (Owing to the antiques and the historic ambience, this inn is not suitable for young children.)

At breakfast innkeeper Gerrie Graham serves Belgian waffles with whipped cream and strawberries or egg dishes with hollandaise. Milt, her husband, a former FBI agent, serves breakfast and helps you plan your day. In the afternoon a tray of tea and cookies is brought to your room.

🏠 *4 doubles with bath, 5 suites. Air-conditioning, TVs, phones in 3 suites. $125–$175; full breakfast, afternoon tea. AE, DC, MC, V. No smoking, no pets.*

Wildflower Inn

167 Palmer Ave., Falmouth 02540, tel. and fax 508/548-9524 or tel. 800/294-5459

The Wildflower Inn first bloomed in 1995, when owners Phil and Donna Stone decided to become innkeepers. They call their decorating style "old made new again": Tables are constructed from early 1900s pedal sewing machine bases; in a former life the living room-breakfast area's sideboard server was a 1920s Hotpoint electric stove; and the antique Hoosier now holds beverages and snacks.

The Stone's innovative decor (and infectious sense of humor) continues in the guest rooms. The Jasmine Room has a safari theme, with soft gold walls, animal wood carvings that have burlap and bamboo accents, and an antique iron four-poster bed with a mosquito-netting canopy. In the skylighted, third-floor, Moonflower Room—where everything is coming up . . . well, sunflowers—the bed is tucked into the eaves so you can count stars instead of sheep. In the attached town house (formerly a stable) the fully furnished Loft Cottage has a spiral staircase that winds up to a bedroom. (Note that although this inn is full of whimsy and humor, it is not suitable for families with young children.)

Donna whips up edible delights using the wildflowers she grows out back. The wraparound porch serves as the summer's breakfast nook; one morning the five-course breakfast might include sunflower crepes or calendula corn muffins—floral feasts that have been featured on the PBS series *Country Inn Cooking*.

▦ *5 doubles with bath, 1 cottage. Air-conditioning, TV in common room, whirlpool baths in 2 rooms, bicycles. $110–$175; full breakfast. AE, MC, V. No smoking, no pets. 2-night minimum weekends and holidays.*

Wingscorton Farm

11 Wing Blvd., East Sandwich 02537, tel. 508/888-0534

This working farm is also an enchanting oasis where you can commune with nature when you're not busy talking (literally) to the animals. A long, winding driveway—sheep on the left, metal pig sculpture on the right, and groves of trees and pastures all around—brings you past a two-bedroom cottage (rented by the week) to the main house, which was built in 1763 and was once a stop on the Underground Railroad.

The dining room has one of the largest fireplaces in New England—the hearth alone is 9-ft long. (When a major snowstorm surprised the Cape back in 1996, owners Sheila Weyers and Richard Loring kept their guests comfy, cozy, and warm!) A richly paneled communal library/den has Asian rugs, wing-back chairs, best-sellers and magazines, and a TV. Each of the four main-house guest suites has a fireplace, braided rugs atop wide-plank floors, wainscoting, and an adjoining smaller bedroom—formerly the birthing rooms. (Today, they hold twin beds and minirefrigerators.)

For privacy (Sheila assures "that only a goat or sheep could spy on you"), request the detached stone carriage house. This honeymooner's haven has a fully equipped kitchen, a living room with a sofa bed and a wood-burning stove, a spiral staircase that leads to a loft bedroom, and a large sundeck. The cottage is fully equipped—perfect for family reunions.

While roaming the 13 acres, expect to run into lots of four-legged critters: the two house dogs, ducks, Genivieve the donkey, chickens (yes, you can help gather eggs), the pair of llamas that occasionally make their presence known, and the various "well-trained" pets brought by guests. The beach is a five-minute walk away. Another favorite feature: the traditional clambakes prepared year-round by visiting members of Martha's Vineyard's Wampanoag tribe.

🏨 *4 suites, carriage house, 2-bedroom cottage. TV in library/den, minirefrigerators, private beach. $115–$200; full breakfast. AE, MC, V. 2-night minimum weekends and holidays.*

Wood Duck Inn

1050 County Rd., Cataumet 02534, tel. 508/564-6404

When Maureen and Dick Jason say they open their 1848 house to guests, they mean it. You can use the living room to entertain or watch TV; if you don't want to use the cooking facilities in your suite, head for the house kitchen. Such friendliness and accessibility add to the pleasure of staying here. Also adding to the unpretentious charm (and something we cannot duck): the myriad duck decoys here, there, and everywhere—especially Dick's hand-carved collectible decoys that are on display (and for sale) in the reception area.

The light, airy Garden and Treetops suites have antiques, handmade quilts, and (of course) decoys. Each also has its own entrance, a sparkling kitchenette, a TV, a sofa bed in the living area, and a bath stocked with bath crystals and oils and plush terry robes. The decks afford idyllic views of conservation lands and cranberry bogs. (Winter guests take note: the bog is ideal for ice-skating or ice sailing.) There's also a small, two-story detached cottage nearby called the Duckling that offers one second-floor suite with a deck and a full kitchen.

🏨 *3 suites, 1 cottage. Air-conditioning in 2 suites; TV, minirefrigerators in all suites; nature trails; ice-skating. $85–$95; Continental-plus breakfast. No credit cards. Smoking in 1 suite. 2-night minimum weekends and holidays in season.*

Martha's Vineyard

Charlotte Inn

Much less developed than mainland Cape Cod, yet more diverse and cosmopolitan than neighboring Nantucket, Martha's Vineyard is an island with a split personality. From Memorial Day through Labor Day the island is a vibrant, star-studded event. Edgartown is flooded with day-trippers who come to wander its tidy streets lined with chic boutiques and stately Federal and Greek Revival homes built by whaling captains. Oak Bluffs has a boardwalk-town atmosphere, with pizza and ice cream shops, a popular dance club, and several bars—all teeming with the high-spirited and the tan.

Multicolor towels blanket the spectacular, miles-long beaches, while the harbors fill with snapping sails and gleaming luxury yachts. Celebrities such as Carly Simon, Sharon Stone, Ted Danson, Patricia Neal, Walter Cronkite, and Diane Sawyer call the island home, either seasonally or year-round. Island concerts, theater, dance, and lectures feature first-rate performers and speakers. Other pleasures include nature preserves, county fairs and festivals, farmers' markets, and fireworks viewed from the Oak Bluffs green.

The Vineyard's summer persona is the one most people come for, but to some, its other self is even more appealing. The off-season island is a place of peace and simple but breathtaking beauty. On drives or bike rides through the agricultural heart of the island, you can linger beside grazing sheep, horses, even llamas in fields bounded by dry stone walls. You can appreciate the lovely beaches in solitude, and the water seems to sparkle more under crisp blue skies.

The locals, too, are at their best in the off-season. After struggling to make the most of the short moneymaking season, they reestablish contact with friends and take up pastimes previously crowded out by work. Cultural, educational, and recreational events are offered year-round, and a number of inns, restaurants, and shops remain open to serve visitors wise enough to seek out the island's quieter charms.

Places to Go, Sights to See

Felix Neck Wildlife Sanctuary. Felix Neck (tel. 508/627–4850), off the Edgartown–Vineyard Haven Road, is laced with 6 mi of self-guided trails that traverse marshland, fields, woods, and seashore. Activities such as guided nature and birding walks are held regularly.

Flying Horses. In Oak Bluffs the many lures for children (an arcade, a slush shop . . .) include an 1876 carousel that still offers the brass ring.

Gay Head Cliffs. These dramatically striated red-clay cliffs at the island's western tip are a major draw, as the parking lot full of buses will attest. The approach to the overlook—from which the Elizabeth Islands are visible across the sound—is lined with shops that sell Native American crafts and fast food. (Gay Head is a Native American township, and in 1997 the town voted to change its name back to Aquinnah, Wampanoag for "land under the hill." Be aware that signs may have both names.)

Menemsha. This little fishing village on the west coast is one of New England's most charming. The jumble of fishing and pleasure boats and of drying lobster pots and nets along the dock may seem familiar—location shots for the movie *Jaws* were filmed here. Besides fish markets and summer boutiques, the village offers a beach (good for sunset picnics), fishing from the jetty, and a seasonal restaurant, *Home Port* (tel. 508/645–2679), with fresh seafood. Save room for an ice cream sundae across the way.

Oak Bluffs Camp Ground. In a little enclave of town, dozens of Carpenter Gothic Victorian cottages, gaily painted and trimmed in lacy filigree, are gathered tightly together, just as the tents they replaced once were. The cottages were built in the late 1800s by Methodists who, in 1835, began to come to the area for a retreat. Oak Bluffs then turned into a popular Victorian summer playground. The spirit of the Camp Meeting is revived in a community sing, held Wednesday nights in season.

Beaches

Joseph Sylvia State Beach, between Oak Bluffs and Edgartown, is a mile-long sandy beach on Nantucket Sound. The calm, warm water makes it popular with families. **Menemsha Beach,** adjacent to the fishing village, is on Vineyard Sound, backed by dunes. Located on the west side of the island, it is a great place to catch the sunset. **South Beach** is a popular 3-mi-long ribbon of sand on the Atlantic, with strong surf and, sometimes, riptides. From Edgartown take the 2-mi bike path to Katama or catch the half-hourly shuttle on Church Street. **Wasque Beach,** on Chappaquiddick Island, is reached via a ferry (it runs from about 7 AM to midnight in season) from Edgartown and then a drive or bike ride east. Part of a wildlife refuge, it offers heavy surf, good bird-watching, and isolation.

Restaurants

Lambert's Cove Country Inn (Lambert Cove Rd., tel. 508/693–2298), in West Tisbury, and the **Beach Plum Inn** (Beach Plum La., tel. 508/645–9454), in Menemsha, offer fine Continental dining in attractive wooded settings. Classic French cuisine—served without pretension and in a casual gardenlike atmosphere—is the bill of fare at **Le Grenier** (96 Main St., tel. 508/693–4906), in Vineyard Haven. Also in Vineyard Haven, the must-visit there-will-always-be-a-line **Black Dog Tavern** (Beach St. Extension, tel. 508/693–9223), perhaps more famous for its T-shirts and sweatshirts emblazoned with the black dog trademark than its food. In Oak Bluffs there's **Zapotec** (10 Kennebec Ave., tel. 508/693–6800), where inexpensive, creative Mexican food is served in an intimate atmosphere.

Nightlife

In 1979 Carly Simon first opened the **Hot Tin Roof** (tel. 508/693–1137), a seasonal nightclub at the Martha's Vineyard Airport, whose roof is, indeed, made of tin. In the summer of 1996 she and three friends joined forces, renovated and reopened the club, and it's hotter than ever. Carly, who took to the stage for the grand reopening, may occasionally perform (unannounced), but usually it's other big names crowding the stage, such as Jimmy Cliff, Hall & Oates, Pat Benatar, and Jerry Lee Lewis. The year-round **Atlantic Connection** (tel. 508/693–7129), in Oak Bluffs, has a fancy light system, live bands (everything from country to Celtic), DJ nights, even karaoke. The nonprofit **Wintertide Coffeehouse** (tel.

508/693–8830) is a year-round smoke- and alcohol-free café-club that dishes out great grub and greater music by the likes of Tom Paxton, Kate Taylor (James's little sister), and Patty Larkin; jazz and jam sessions; and comedy and open-mike nights.

Reservations Services

Any Day Reservations (tel. 508/696–9990 or 888/633–3700 in MA or CT), **House Guests Cape Cod and the Islands** (Box 1881, Orleans 02653, tel. 508/896–7053 or 800/666–4678), **Martha's Vineyard and Nantucket Reservations** (Box 1322, Vineyard Haven 02568, tel. 508/693–7200 or 800/649–5671 in MA).

Visitor Information

Martha's Vineyard Chamber of Commerce (Beach Rd., Box 1698, Vineyard Haven 02568, tel. 508/693–0085).

Admiral Benbow Inn

81 New York Ave. (Box 2488), Oak Bluffs 02557, tel. 508/693-6825, fax 508/693-1131

Separated from the busy road between Vineyard Haven and Oak Bluffs by a white picket fence and a tree-shaded lawn, this homey B&B, converted in 1985, remains much as it was when it was built for a minister at the turn of the century. Throughout the house the elaborate woodwork has been preserved. The Victorian parlor has a stunning nonworking fireplace, with a frame of carved wood and ceramic bas-relief.

The guest rooms (try to avoid a room on the side facing the gas station) are furnished in a pleasant hodgepodge of antiques, including brass beds and some Victorian pieces. Victorian-inspired wallpapers add to the period feel. In the country-style formal dining room, innkeeper Joyce Dodge, who took over the inn in 1996, serves a Continental-plus breakfast.

▥ *6 doubles with bath, 1 suite. Ceiling fans, TV in sitting room. $120-$175; Continental-plus breakfast. AE, D, MC, V. Smoking in common room, no pets. 2-night minimum weekends, 3-night minimum holidays. Closed Dec.–Apr.*

The Bayberry

Old Courthouse Rd. (Box 654), West Tisbury 02575, tel. 508/693-1984

A stay at this Cape-style house with peaked roof and weathered gray shingles about 5 mi outside Vineyard Haven is like a visit to Grandma's. Innkeeper Rosalie Powell displays her many antiques collections—majolica, baskets, pewter—in her comfortable living room, where you can relax by the fireplace, play the piano, or read before a bay window looking onto 4 acres surrounded by meadows and woods. (Preteens may not appreciate the peaceful atmosphere

here; it's best to leave the young ones at home.)

Guest rooms have some antiques—a marble-top dresser, a rolltop desk, a four-poster pineapple bed—and such homey touches as handmade quilts and rugs. The only thing fancy about this B&B is the breakfast, served in the fireplace-warmed country kitchen on antique pine tables set with linens, candles, and blue-and-white Staffordshire china. In nice weather you can take breakfast on the backyard patio with birdsong as background music. Entrées such as French toast with grilled bananas and Grand Marnier sauce are accompanied by warm popovers and breads.

▥ *3 doubles with bath, 2 doubles share bath. Guest refrigerator, croquet, beach passes and towels. $100-$150; full breakfast, afternoon tea. MC, V. No smoking, no pets. 2-night minimum weekends.*

Beach Plum Inn and Cottages

Beach Plum La. off North Rd., Menemsha 02552, tel. 508/645-9454, fax 508/645-2801

This 10-acre retreat's main attractions are a secluded woodland setting, a panoramic view of Menemsha Harbor, and a romantic upscale restaurant with windows that take advantage of the view (be sure to reserve a table for a time when you can catch one of the spectacular sunsets). Owners Paul and Janie Darrow preside at an afternoon cocktail hour on the lawn.

Guest rooms—some with private decks and great views—have eclectic, modern touches, including hand-painted pieces, small new baths, and wall-to-wall carpeting. The cottages, scattered among the trees, are decorated in casual beach style, with wicker or other simple furnishings.

▥ *5 doubles with bath, 4 1- or 2-bedroom cottages with bath. Restaurant,* air-conditioning in some rooms, beach passes, bike rentals, tennis, croquet, baby-sitting, turndown service. $175–$300; full breakfast. AE, D, MC, V. No smoking, no pets. 4-night minimum in season. Closed Nov.–Apr.

Charlotte Inn

27 S. Summer St., Edgartown 02539, tel. 508/627–4751, fax 508/627–4652

On a quiet street in the center of well-groomed Edgartown is an inn that stands out like a polished gem. Gery Conover, owner for more than 20 years, and his wife, Paula, oversee every detail with meticulous care and obvious pride. From the original structure, an 1860 white-clapboard home that belonged to a whaling-company owner, the Charlotte has grown into a five-building complex connected by lawns and a courtyard. Ivy-bordered brick walkways lead past pockets of garden to flower-filled nooks perfect for reading or reflection. Across the street is the early 18th-century Garden House; one gorgeous room has French doors that open to a terrace that looks onto a large English garden.

True Anglophiles, the Conovers have furnished the inn through antiquing trips to England—and continue to do so, since each room is redone completely every five years. Guest rooms feature mahogany furniture; brass lamps; original art; richly colored wallpapers; lush fabrics; and down-filled pillows, comforters, and chair cushions. One room in the veranda-wrapped 1850 Summer House has a fireplace and a baby grand piano.

The most exquisite accommodations on the island are here, in the Coach House. Set above a re-created estate garage lined with gleaming natural wood walls, the suite has cathedral ceilings, a Palladian window, French doors, a green marble fireplace, and sumptuous furnishings. Everywhere you look there's something wonderful: sterling silver lamps, Minton bone china, white cutwork bed linens.

The main inn's ground floor is spacious and elegant, with sporting and marine art and contemporary works displayed throughout. The mahogany-paneled common room with a fireplace draws guests for afternoon tea and cocktails. In winter breakfast is served there on white-cloth-covered tables. (Note that the atmosphere here is not conducive to the patter of little feet.)

The fine restaurant L'étoile, set in a glassed-in summerhouse, is open for dinner and Sunday brunch. It mixes luxuriant greenery, spotlighted oil paintings, and surprising antique accents, such as leather-bound books perched on the rafters. The contemporary French menu highlights local seafood and game.

▥ *23 doubles with bath, 2 suites. Restaurant, air-conditioning, TV in all rooms, phones in most rooms. $250–$650; Continental breakfast, afternoon tea. AE, MC, V. No pets. 2-night minimum weekends, 3-night minimum holidays. Restaurant closed Jan.–mid-Feb.*

Crocker House Inn

12 Crocker Ave., Vineyard Haven 02568 tel. 508/693–1151 or 800/772–0206

On a quiet street that dead-ends with a town beach, this lavender and periwinkle fantasy is a short stroll from downtown Vineyard Haven. The house has eight guest rooms, each crowned with owner Darlene Stavens's touches of whimsy. The first-floor Lace Room, boldly painted in purple, has a working fireplace, a queen-size brass bed, antique furniture, and lots o' lace—including an antique wedding veil hanging on a wall. (No wonder Darlene urges lovers to stay here—where better to pop the question?)

If it's space you want, then request the third-floor Loft Room, which is reached via a steep staircase. It has a nautical theme and a sitting area, a private entrance, a balcony with a water view, skylights that flood the room with sunlight, and a bath with a claw-foot tub. (This inn is not suitable for young children.)

🏠 *8 doubles with bath. Air-conditioning, minirefrigerator in 1 room and common area, beach access, free parking (first-come, first-served basis). $85–$160; Continental-plus breakfast. AE, MC, V. No smoking, no pets. 3-night minimum weekends and holidays. Closed Nov.– Mar.*

The Daggett House

59 N. Water St. (Box 1333), Edgartown 02539, tel. 508/627–4600 or 800/946–3400, fax 508/627–4611

The flower-bordered lawn that separates the main house from the harbor makes a great retreat after a day of exploring the town, a minute away. The circa 1660 Colonial house—with weathered gray shingles, a white picket fence, and a lavish garden—incorporates a tavern and breakfast room, open to the public year-round. Much of its historical ambience has been preserved, including a secret stairway that's now a private entrance to an upstairs guest room.

All three inn buildings—including the Captain Warren House across the street and a three-room cottage between the main house and the water—are decorated with fine wallpapers, antiques, and reproductions (some canopy beds). The Widow's Walk Suite has a rooftop hot tub with a great view of Edgartown Harbor, as well as a formal dining room and a kitchen; another suite has a hot tub on a private water-view balcony. If you're lucky, maybe you'll spot the resident ghost—one guest caught the spirited spirit on film; the evidence hangs in the common room.

🏠 *19 doubles and 1 single with bath (1 double has a kitchenette), 4 suites. Restaurant, air-conditioning in 3 rooms, cable TV and phones in all rooms, beach towels, laundry service. $145–$395. AE, D, MC, V. No smoking, no pets. 2-night minimum May–Oct.*

Duck Inn

State Rd. (Box 160), Gay Head 02535, tel. 508/645–9018

Innkeeper-owner Elise LeBovit will freely admit that she is daffy over ducks. It shows—from the Daffy Duck place mats to the quacking phone to the signs that warn guests to DUCK when using the narrow staircases. But Elise is also daffy over eccentricity—the five guest rooms and all the common areas in this 200-year-old masterpiece are decorated in a style that could only be described as eclectic. The common Santa Fe Room, for example, is an explosion of clutter and confusion, as well as a nod to all things Navajo—stucco walls, Native American rugs and blankets and terracotta pottery. The Q (as in "quack") Room is a Far East wonder, with silk kimonos hanging on the walls and rice-paper lamps. Other rooms pay homage to Art Deco, English country, and Cape Cod styles. The sunporch has glorious views of the Gay Head Lighthouse and the multicolored Gay Head Cliffs.

A winding stone staircase takes you to the inn's only suite, literally carved into the house's 2-ft-thick granite foundation (carried to the site by oxen and the house's builder, a Native American whaler named George Belain). There's a queen-size bedroom here as well as a sitting area with a fireplace and a sofa bed. Outside the private entrance sits the communal hot tub. A masseuse is available for facials or body rubs.

Health-conscious Elise serves a breakfast that is good—and good for you— with such house "organic gourmet" specialties as pear couscous muffins and chocolate raspberry crepes. (Elise will accommodate special diets.) Don't be surprised to find the house pets begging for a taste, including Orally, a very large, very friendly, very noisy Vietnamese pot-bellied pig.

🏠 *4 doubles share 3 baths, 1 suite. TV in suite and common room, phones in*

all rooms, hot tub, beach access. $95–
$175; full breakfast. MC, V. No smoking
in common room, pets allowed in suite
and 1 other room.

Greenwood House

40 Greenwood Ave., Vineyard Haven
02568, tel. 508/693–6150 or 800/525–9466,
fax 508/696–8113

This small, mustard-color, shingled B&B
sits in a residential, turn-of-the-century
section of town. The four guest rooms
are decorated simply and similarly, with
quilts, floral-print wallpaper, canopy and
four-poster beds, and Victorian period
reproduction furniture. Each room also
has a minirefrigerator, a phone, cable
TV, a clock radio, air-conditioning, and
private bath replete with hair dryer.

The sunny, white-walled common sitting
room leads into a formal dining room,
where a Continental-plus breakfast is
served. Off the kitchen is an inviting, enclosed sunporch whose wicker furnishings and cedar-shingle walls add to the
breezy, carefree feeling.

Proprietors Kathy Stinson and Larry
Gomez, who have been running the
Greenwood since 1994, strictly enforce
their no-smoking rule: Smoking is pro-
hibited inside and outside on the grounds!

▥ 1 double with bath, 3 suites. Air-conditioning, cable TV, phones, minirefrigerators, hair dryers in rooms; croquet.
$159–$239; Continental-plus breakfast.
AE, DC, MC, V. No smoking, no pets,
children allowed only in 1 room. 3-night
minimum weekends and holidays.

Lambert's Cove
Country Inn

Lambert's Cove Rd., R.R. 1 (Box 422),
West Tisbury 02575, tel. 508/693–2298,
fax 508/693–7890

Approached via a narrow, winding road
through pine woods, this secluded re-

treat is everything a country inn should
be. The 1790 farmhouse is set amid an
apple orchard, a large English garden
bordered by lilac bushes, and woods that
hide a tennis court. In spring an ancient
tree is draped in blossoms from 20-ft wisteria vines (a popular photo spot for the
many weddings held here); in fall a Con-
cord grape arbor scents the air.

The inn's common areas are elegant yet
welcoming, with rich woodwork and
large flower arrangements. In the large,
airy, gentleman's library, part of the additions made in the 1920s, you'll find
book-lined white walls, a fireside group-
ing of upholstered wing chairs, rich red
Asian carpets on a polished wood floor,
and French doors that open to the orchard. A cozier reading area on the second-floor landing offers a sofa and
shelves of books and magazines.

The guest rooms are in the main house
and in two adjacent buildings. Most
main-house rooms have a soft, soothing
country look framed by Laura Ashley
wallpapers; two at the back can be converted to a suite with a connecting sitting room that has a sofa bed and sliders
opening onto a backyard deck. Rooms in
the other houses are more rustic. Two
rooms upstairs in the Barn have exposed
beams; downstairs one large room with
a sofa bed has sliders out to a deck. The
Carriage House has camp-style decks
and screened porches. Comfort is the
focus, meaning unfussy furnishings; firm
beds with country quilts; and bright,
cheerful baths with plush towels.

Fine dining is part of the experience,
and the romantic restaurant serves unpretentious Continental cuisine in an intimate atmosphere of soft lighting and
music. The innkeepers since 1996 are
Louis and Katherine Costabel; he is an
awarding-winning Cordon Bleu chef.

▥ 15 doubles with bath. Restaurant
(dinner and Sun. brunch; off-season,
weekends only), air-conditioning in
some rooms, TV in common room, beach
passes, tennis court. $125–$175; Continental breakfast. AE, MC, V. No smok-

*ing in common areas, no pets. 3-night
minimum July–Aug.*

Oak House

*Sea View Ave. (Box 299), Oak Bluffs
02557, tel. 508/693–4187, fax 508/696–
7385*

Among the summer homes along the
coast road just outside Oak Bluffs center stands the Oak House B&B. Built in
1872 and enlarged and lavishly refurbished in the early 1900s, this wonderful
Victorian beach house features a playful
gingerbread-trimmed pastel facade and
a wraparound veranda with much-used
rockers and even a swing or two.

Inside the reason for the inn's name becomes clear: Everywhere you look, you
see richly patinated oak: in ceilings, wall
paneling, wainscoting, and furnishings.
The two bedrooms that constitute the
Captain's Room are fitted out like ship
cabins and have oak wainscoted walls
and ceilings. The best of the rooms with
balconies (large enough for two chairs)
is the Governor Claflin Room; its French
doors open wide to let in a broad expanse
of sea and sky. Unfortunately, cars whiz
past on the road below, which some people may find distracting.

When the Convery family bought the
Oak House in 1988, they created several
tiny bathrooms out of existing closets.
One spacious hall bath, with peach-
painted pressed-tin walls and ceiling, a
dressing table, and the inn's only tub,
was turned into a private bath for the
very feminine Tivoli Room.

Alison Convery's island antiques shops
provided much of the inn's superb furniture, brass lamps, sea chests, and such.
The entrance hall evokes an elegant Victorian home, with high ceilings, a baby
grand piano, a hand-cranked organ, potted palms, and an impressive central
staircase lined with sumptuous red
Asian carpeting. The sunporch has lots
of white wicker, plants, floral print pillows, and original stained-glass window

accents. (With so many antiques here,
it's best to leave the wee ones at home.)

In the afternoon guests wander back
from the beach (across the street) to
chat. Homemade lemonade and iced tea,
along with elegant tea cakes and cookies,
are provided by Alison's daughter, Betsi
Convery-Luce, the warm and open
innkeeper and a Cordon Bleu–trained
pastry chef.

🏠 *8 doubles with bath, 2 suites. Air-
conditioning in 4 rooms; TV in common
room, some rooms, and both suites;
beach access. $130–$225; Continental
breakfast, afternoon tea. AE, D, MC, V.
No pets. 3-night minimum weekends
and holidays in season. Closed mid-
Oct.–early May.*

Outermost Inn

*Lighthouse Rd. (R.R. 1, Box 171), Gay
Head 02535, tel. 508/645–3511, fax 508/
645–3514*

In 1990 Hugh and Jeanne Taylor (he's
singing James's brother) finished converting the sprawling, gray-shingle
home they built 20 years ago—and are
raising their two children in—into a
B&B. Hugh's redesign takes full advantage of the superb location, at the
sparsely populated westernmost end of
the island. Standing alone on acres of
wide-open moorland, the two-story
house is wrapped with picture windows
that reveal breathtaking views; to the
north are the Elizabeth Islands and, beyond, mainland Cape Cod. The sweeping
red and white beams of the Gay Head
Lighthouse, just over the moors on the
Gay Head Cliffs, add a touch of romance
at night. (Indeed, the atmosphere here
is more suited to couples than to families
with young children.)

White walls and polished light-wood
floors of ash, cherry, beech, oak, and hick-
ory create a bright, clean setting for simple contemporary-style furnishings and
local art. Fabrics used throughout the
inn are all natural—in the dhurrie rugs,

the down-filled cotton comforters, and the all-cotton sheets. Several corner rooms offer window walls on two sides. The Lighthouse Suite has a private entrance, a skylighted bath, and a separate living room with a butcher-block dining table. The Oak Room has French doors that open onto a deck with a great view.

The porch, set with hammocks and rocking chairs, is ideal for relaxing and watching birds and deer. Breakfast is served there or in the dining room, which has a fireplace and window wall. In the afternoon complimentary hors d'oeuvres and setups for drinks are provided on request. During peak season the inn operates a restaurant (by reservation only) that offers a mix of gourmet and home cooking prepared by a Culinary Institute–trained chef—another excuse for you not to wander far from the nest.

When you are ready to venture out, the owners are happy to help with arrangements for all kinds of activities. Hugh has sailed the local waters since childhood, and he will charter out his 50-ft catamaran for excursions to Cuttyhunk Island. There's a privately accessed beach just a five-minute walk away.

🏠 *6 doubles with bath, 1 suite. Restaurant (in season), phones, beach passes. $210–$240; full breakfast. AE, MC, V. Smoking only on porch, no pets. 2-night minimum weekends.*

Sea Spray Inn

2 Nashawena Park (Box 2125), Oak Bluffs 02557, tel. 508/693-9388

In 1989 artist and art restorer Rayeanne King converted her Victorian summerhouse into a B&B that still feels like a summerhouse. It is in a quiet spot in Oak Bluffs, on a drive circling an open, grassy park by the bike path and road that lead to Edgartown. Beyond the park, and just a few minutes' walk from the inn, is a sandy ocean beach. Public tennis and golf are also within walking distance.

The decor is simple and restful (best to leave the kids at home), highlighted by cottage antiques and cheerful splashes of color, including furniture and floors painted in lavender, baby blue, and pink. In the Honeymoon Room an iron-and-brass bed is positioned for watching the sunrise through bay windows draped in lacy curtains; the cedar-lined bath has an extralarge shower. The Garden Room has a king-size bed with a gauze canopy and an enclosed porch.

There are plenty of places to lounge, either on the wide wraparound porch, set with rockers and wicker and looking onto the park, or in the lovely, airy living room.

🏠 *5 doubles with bath, 2 doubles share bath. TV in common room, barbecue grill. $75–$130; Continental breakfast. MC, V. No smoking, no pets. 3-night minimum July–Aug., 2-night minimum weekends in peak season. Closed mid-Nov.–mid-Apr.*

Shiverick Inn

Corner of Pease's Point Way and Pent La. (Box 640), Edgartown 02539, tel. 508/627-3797 or 800/723-4292, fax 508/627-8441

Staying at this grand 1840 house with mansard roof and cupola is like staying at an elegant private residence. The American and English 18th- and 19th-century furnishings throughout are exceptional. Rich fabrics and wallpapers and such accents as Asian rugs, gilt-edged mirrors, cut-glass lamps, and antique art are impeccably chosen. (Note that the atmosphere here is not suitable for young children.)

The inn was bought in April 1992 by Denny and Marty Turmelle, who left corporate careers in Manchester, New Hampshire, to become innkeepers. One or the other presides over breakfast, which is served on china and crystal in a lovely summerhouse-style room with a wood-burning fireplace. Off the second-floor library is a terrace with a pretty view of a white steepled church; a flagstone patio has a small garden.

🎴 *10 doubles with bath, 1 sitting room connects to 1 or 2 adjacent rooms to form a suite. Air-conditioning, TV in library, bicycle rentals. $170–$225; Continental breakfast. AE, D, MC, V. No smoking, no pets.*

Thorncroft Inn

460 Main St. (Box 1022), Vineyard Haven 02568, tel. 508/693-3333 or 800/ 332-1236, fax 508/693-5419

Set amid 3½ wooded acres about a mile from town and the Vineyard Haven ferry, the Thorncroft seems a piece of English countryside. Beyond a manicured lawn bordered in neat boxwood hedges and flowering shrubs is the tidy Craftsman bungalow—gray-green with white shutters and a dormered second story—that was built in 1918 as the guest house of a large estate.

Since they bought the place in 1981, Karl and Lynn Buder have renovated it from top to bottom, furnishing it beautifully with a mix of antiques and reproductions to create an environment that is elegant yet soothing. In addition, they built a Carriage House that has five double rooms geared for romance, with large whirlpool baths (backed with mirrored alcoves) and fireplaces. Two other irresistible rooms have private hot-tub rooms with screens just under the roof that let in fresh air for an alpine effect.

Considering Lynn's master's degree in business administration and Karl's in public administration, it is not surprising that the Thorncroft—now their only business—is run so efficiently. The fine Colonial and richly carved Renaissance Revival antiques are meticulously maintained. Beds are firm, floors thickly carpeted, tiled bathrooms modern and well lighted. Room fireplaces are piled with logs and kindling each day, ready for the touch of a match. Ice buckets, wine

glasses, and corkscrews are provided in each guest room, as is a notebook of information on the area. The bedrooms are wired for computer modems—for those who just *can't* leave work behind. And for those who can, there's a bookcase full of magazines on an amazing range of subjects. There's also a wicker sunporch in which to read them, if you like.

You can have a Continental breakfast delivered to your room and set up elegantly on table-height trays, or you can sign up for one of two seatings the night before. A bell calls you to the table, where you can exchange touring tips with other guests over such entrées as almond French toast and Belgian waffles.

🎴 *14 doubles with bath. Minirefrigerators in some rooms; air-conditioning, bathrobes, hair dryers, irons, cable TV, phones in all rooms; whirlpool baths in 5 rooms; hot tubs in 2 rooms; complimentary morning newspaper. $150– $450; full breakfast, afternoon tea. AE, D, DC, MC, V. No smoking, no pets, children allowed in 1 room only.*

Victorian Inn

24 S. Water St., Edgartown 02539, tel. 508/627-4784

A circa 1820 whaling captain's home listed on the National Register of Historic Places, this ornate Victorian has fish-scale shingling and a mansard roof. New owners Stephen and Karyn Caliri, who have happily returned to small-town life after working in psychology and finance, are thoroughly engaged in renovation. They have imported cast-iron fireplaces from England for the dining room and parlor and built arched brick steps to the patio; in the guest rooms their improvement work continues.

The five spacious third-floor guest rooms have high ceilings and French doors that lead to balconies—some with a view of the harbor and Chappaquiddick. Six other guest rooms have a mix of antiques and reproductions, with some canopy and four-poster beds, in the Empire or Federal style. Each room also has ceiling fans and decanters of cream sherry. All the bathrooms have been redone with glass-door shower stalls and floral wallpaper or neutral walls and black and white tile floors. (Couples and families with older children will be more comfortable at this inn than will families with young children.)

In summer breakfast—your choice of two entrées (such as eggs or pancakes) as well as fresh fruit, cereal, and muffins—is served in a courtyard that's shaded by trees and has an arbor laced with morning glories and wisteria. In colder weather breakfast is served in front of the dining room fireplace.

▦ *14 doubles with bath. $110–$225; full breakfast, afternoon tea. AE, MC, V. No smoking, pets allowed in off-season. 2-night minimum weekends, 3-night minimum holidays.*

Nantucket

Ten Lyon Street Inn

At the height of its prosperity, in the early to mid-19th century, the little island of Nantucket became the foremost whaling port in the world. Before the boom years ended, some of the hard-won profits went into the building of grand homes that still survive. Indeed, Nantucket town hardly seems changed since its whaling days; its cobblestone streets remain lighted by old-fashioned street lamps, and its hundreds of 17th- to 19th-century houses—with weathered gray shingles or clapboard painted white or gray—have been beautifully preserved.

Hard times must take their share of the credit for this preservation—after the boom came the bust, when there was no money to tear down and rebuild and, in fact, few residents left to do it. Still, Nantucket's past has also been kept alive through conscious effort. A very strict code now regulates any structural changes within the town, which is part of a national historic district that encompasses most of the island. The code's success is obvious in a restful harmony of architectural styles. When the neat gardens are in bloom and the houses are blanketed with cascading pink roses, it all seems perfect.